Praise for *Don't Send Him*

Jarlath O'Brien has lifted the cloak on the i.̱___ tem. With a humbling combination of academic rigour and deep passion and care for children, he shines a light on the thousands of children who should have a better deal than they do. But what is so uplifting about this book is that it is filled with stories of how pupils, supported by their teachers and other professionals, have achieved extraordinary things. At times, it challenged me to think about my own leadership and what I could have done differently. This is a must-read for all those leading schools today.

Andy Buck, Managing Director of Leadership Matters, author and speaker

In intricate detail, drawn from profound personal and professional experiences, O'Brien paints a picture of a special needs system rapidly running out of options. With urgency and acuity he sets out imperatives for government, school leaders, teachers and agencies to build a future for those young people whose entitlement should be, but isn't yet, the most accepted truth.

Barney Angliss, Special Needs Jungle

This forthright book is a must for every staffroom. It shines a light on the shortcomings of the education system for children with SEN. It highlights inequalities, whilst going a long way to bringing these valuable yet vulnerable members of our communities out of the shadows.

Jarlath is honest about his own professional failings in the past, as he seeks to educate other teachers by example and create a culture where SEN is everybody's business.

Until a holistic approach to understanding the uniqueness of each pupil, and how their strengths can be developed and celebrated, is implemented we will never move beyond mere labels.

This is truly a book that will galvanise change.

Hayley Goleniowska, parent, speaker, former SEN assistant and author

This is a hard-hitting and timely read at a moment of intense educational change that affects all children – including those with special educational needs and disabilities. Jarlath pulls no punches when he sets out the current situation and future prospects for the most vulnerable young people in our society and demands change from policy makers, school leaders and local authorities.

This book is well-researched, and full of real examples that give meat to the bones of a disturbing story that challenges us in the way that we as a society treat our weakest members and their families.

Everyone who has an interest in education, particularly school leaders and policy makers, should read this book – because a good education, one that prepares young people for adult life, belongs to all our children.

Nancy Gedge, SEN teacher and *TES* columnist

I have long enjoyed Jarlath O'Brien's wit and style, and this book is no exception. The author has a winning formula of anecdote and gossip, rooted in deep experience, reflection and research.

Roy Blatchford CBE, Founding Director, National Education Trust

Extremely considered, reflective and honest, *Don't Send Him in Tomorrow* is a thought-provoking and informative read for anyone who has experience of the education of people with learning disabilities. Perhaps more importantly, it is an essential read for anyone who doesn't.

Simon Knight, Deputy Head Teacher, Frank Wise School

Jarlath O'Brien

Don't Send Him in Tomorrow

Shining a light on the marginalised, disenfranchised and forgotten children of today's schools

Independent Thinking Press

First published by

Independent Thinking Press
Crown Buildings, Bancyfelin, Carmarthen, Wales, SA33 5ND, UK
www.independentthinkingpress.com

Independent Thinking Press is an imprint of Crown House Publishing Ltd.

First published 2016.

The extract on pp. 51—52 © Telegraph Media Group Limited, 2016 and has been reproduced with permission.
The extract on p. 75 has been reproduced with kind permission of Kristian Still.
The extract on p. 105 has been reproduced with kind permission of Jules Daulby.
The extract on pp. 152—153 originally appeared in the *TES* and is reproduced with kind permission.

Edited by Ian Gilbert

British Library Cataloguing-in-Publication Data
A catalogue entry for this book is available from the British Library.

Print ISBN 978-178135253-3
Mobi ISBN 978-178135261-8
ePub ISBN 978-178135262-5
ePDF ISBN 978-178135263-2

Printed and bound in the UK by TJ International Ltd, Padstow, Cornwall

For Uncle Thomas (1948–1984) who, I have only recently realised, taught me all those years ago that perfect love casts out fear.

Contents

Acknowledgements

Thanks go to:

Emma, Aidan and Hannah, for showing me what really matters.

Alex Ewen, for being the first follower.

Debra Bratt, Brad Goodwin, Tim Novis, Eddie Owen, Antony Power and Kim Walker, for being the epitome of modest, professional volunteers and for their gentle, yet persistent, hands in the small of my back.

The parents who agreed to talk to me about their experiences in preparation for writing this book. I am grateful to them for their candour, and they should know that I take significant professional sustenance from their tenacity and dignity. The accounts involving parents and children have been anonymised but their stories have been faithfully told here, either as they were recounted to me or as I have witnessed first-hand.

Ian Gilbert, for encouraging me to put pen to paper and for caring about and seeing this group of young people.

The inspiring band of people all over the world who dedicate their lives to working with children and adults with learning difficulties, and who are a joy to work with.

The staff, students, parents and governors of Carwarden House Community School, Haybrook College and Holyport Manor School (now Manor Green School), for teaching me far more than I ever taught them.

Foreword by Timothy Novis

'Monday's child is fair of face
Tuesday's child is full of grace,
Wednesday's child is full of woe,
Thursday's child has *far to go...*'

My daughter Vivian was born on a Thursday, and I can remember that night with chilling clarity. As the doctor held her towards my mother-in-law, I could see a mutual look of concern tinged with an antiseptic certainty, and then their eyes turned to me, and turned downwards.

Then it was home for the agonising wait for the results of the blood tests and the empirical evidence, as scientific as it was undeniable, that she has an extra pod on her twenty-first chromosome – Trisomy 21 – Down syndrome.

My first telephone call, in an attempt to assuage my own anxieties, was to my spiritual director – a much wiser and somewhat older fellow priest with whom I regularly met. 'In a year from now, you'll tell me what a blessing she is.' It didn't take a year. Very quickly, Vivian established herself in a very special place in my heart and in the hearts of so many others. She was to be a violet in a field of daisies. She was the ticket we bought to vacation in one particular place, only to discover we were to be taken by forces beyond our control somewhere very different indeed, but yet no less amazing. We had just received membership in a club we really hadn't ever thought about joining.

If I were to describe my outlook on life as a kind of Venn diagram, my three conjoined circles would be titled 'Dad', 'Chaplain' and 'Chair'. Vivian's proud Dad. The Chaplain at Wellington College. And Chair of the Board of Governors of Vivian's amazing school – Carwarden House. And of course, at the centre of my Venn diagram, is Vivian herself – informing, enriching and enlivening all my other roles.

But until I happened upon being in such a close relationship with a child with special needs, I was like the thousands of others who never really saw such children or knew anything about them. I took the attitude that 'children are an investment in the future', and failed to see that such an approach looked at the younger generations in terms of a kind of economic transaction – what we put in will be paid back with interest. I didn't realise that I tended to see people as a means to an end, rather than as ends unto themselves. And that really, all of us are human *beings*, and were never meant to be merely human *doings*.

I suspect that departments of education throughout the world really struggle with those attitudes towards our children. When making policy, that is the lens through which they make sense of their decisions.

Children with special needs force us to change reading glasses. Even just to move around the room and sit in a different chair to gain a new perspective. And that is their very gift.

If we do, as Jarlath so wisely recommends, shine a light on them, we will come to realise that it is really they who exude their own light, who call us, 'average people', out of the shadows and into a deeper understanding of – you name it.

Vivian, my violet, is a bright light in her own special way. I wouldn't have said that on that baffling Thursday, 16 years ago.

Father Timothy Novis is chaplain at Wellington College

Introduction

'The moral test of government is how it treats those who are in the dawn of life, the children; those who are in the twilight of life, the aged; and those in the shadows of life, the sick, the needy and the handicapped.'

Hubert Humphrey,
former Vice-President of the United States of America (remarks at the dedication of the Hubert H. Humphrey Building, 1 November 1977)

One of the occupational hazards of the life of a teacher is the inadvertent encounter with a student outside school: the crossing of paths in the bread aisle at the supermarket or, more surprisingly when it happened to me, in Macy's department store in New York one bitter February half-term. It can be uncomfortable for both student and teacher; the teacher's internal computer instantly reverts to work mode and, usually depending on the age of the child, they are either delighted or horrified to run into someone who doesn't exist in their mind beyond the boundary of the school gates.

How was it possible, then, for me to live within 50 metres of Sean, one of my students, for two years before I became aware of it? Our finely tuned radar will normally spot a child from school long before they have seen us. If a student lived at the bottom of the street, you'd know about it, surely?

I discovered that Sean and I are neighbours when I was signing off the paperwork for the annual review of his statement of special educational needs (SEN). The address caught my eye as I was sure it contained a typing error – he couldn't possibly live there; I'd know about it. How could a student in my school live within shouting distance of my front door and yet be invisible to both me and the local community? A moment's thought told me why.

Sean has profound and multiple learning difficulties. He relies entirely on adult support to survive. He is tube-fed. He is incontinent. Sean has very limited fine motor skills. He can communicate in two ways: he can point with his eyes to indicate a preference for one of two simple choices, such as a choice of food, and he will cry when he is unhappy.

I used to leave for work at 7am, whereas Sean would be collected by a specially converted minibus an hour later. Sean would leave school at 3.30pm, whereas I would remain at school for some hours afterwards, getting home long after him. If you happened to be passing his house at pick-up or drop-off time you might catch sight of him. At all other times he was totally out of sight and, therefore, out of mind.

Sean, now in his early twenties, and I are still neighbours. I have lived in our village for nine years now and have *never* seen Sean there. Had I not seen Sean's address on that document I would still be blissfully unaware that we live in such close proximity. As I write this, sitting on the sofa in my living room, I can see the entire street, but I can't see him. To all intents and purposes, he is invisible.

Sean was the epitome of the invisible child, but unfortunately he is not the only one. There is a group of young people in this country who are effectively invisible to the rest of society. They are not with their friends in a coffee shop doing their homework after school; they are not in the local football team; they aren't playing in the street with their friends on their bikes at the weekend; they are not in the school play; they are not at a sleepover on a Saturday night; they aren't invited to birthday parties.

This group is not just defined by some profound disability; the group is larger and more diverse than that. They are invisible. Their needs are made invisible. Comments like 'There's no such thing as attention deficit hyperactivity disorder (ADHD), just bad parenting,' and 'Pathological demand avoidance (PDA) just means a kid who doesn't like to be told "no"', are statements I've heard many times, and they never fail to irritate me. Imagine the impact of those statements on the parents of such a child.

Not only are their needs denied, but their ambitions are then stunted by barely believable Henry Ford-inspired school policies such as streamed option booklets for Year 9s. (You can choose any subject you like, as long as it's not history.)

Then their social development is impeded by the creation of separate play areas at break and lunch times. Worse still is when parents are strong-armed into collecting their child to take them home for lunch. Even their domestic circumstances are invisible, unless they are highlighted and then mocked in a Channel 4 documentary or a *Daily Mail* headline.

This invisibility suits society in the same way that we prefer the elderly, those with dementia, asylum-seekers or prisoners to be cared for, managed, kept away, locked up or just made to disappear.

Even politicians, whose role it is to fight for every member of society, seem unable to acknowledge their existence. 'We will expect *every* pupil by the age of 11 to know their times tables off by heart, to perform long division and complex multiplication, and to be able to read a novel,' said Nicky Morgan, the then Secretary of State for Education, in February 2015 (emphasis added).[1]

The achievements of this group of young people count for as close as it is possible to get to zero. They are marginalised, disenfranchised and, ultimately, forgotten.

These children are in your classroom. They are in your school. Yet the way our education system, and society more widely, is currently organised makes it very difficult for them to be seen, let alone thrive.

We have taken action, and rightly so, to promote the achievement of children who are in the care of local authorities, the group with the poorest academic outcomes of all. This has manifested itself in mandatory completion of six-monthly Personal Education Plans (PEPs) by an equally mandatory 'designated teacher for looked-after children'. Note that PEPs are completed more frequently than annual reviews of the statements or Education, Health and Care Plans (EHCPs) of children with SEN. Schools or local authorities (it varies by region, as some local authorities retain control over this money) also receive £1,900 per child who is currently looked-after or has been adopted. Each local authority has a so-called Virtual School for Looked-After Children, with a head teacher who could reasonably be considered to be the champion of these children in that part of the world.

This is great and how it should be, in theory at least. However, no such post exists for children with learning difficulties.

We have taken action, again with clear justification, for children who are living in poverty and who are, as a result, entitled to free school meals. Schools receive money, known as the Pupil Premium and currently set at £1,320 for each child in primary schools and £935 for each child in secondary schools (but not beyond Year 11, interestingly). Schools are required to produce an annual Pupil Premium Report accounting for how they have spent this money and the effectiveness of that expenditure. Failure to show that this disadvantaged group are catching up with their peers (colloquially known as 'closing the gap') can sink a school in an Ofsted inspection. This action went as far as the then Minister of State for Schools, David Laws, who wrote to individual schools congratulating them on their successes with this group of children. I am sure that those schools are justifiably proud of those achievements, but similar letters from a minister to schools lauding the achievements of their children with learning difficulties are conspicuous by their absence. To be a school that has a strong reputation for giving a massive boost to the life chances of children living in poverty is clearly a desirable thing. I suspect that there are some schools that do not want a similar reputation for their work with children with learning difficulties.

Why is this?

The cohort of children who qualify for free school meals is dictated by a school's catchment. Parents of those children do not suddenly gravitate towards another school in the same town because of its reputation for doing great things with this cohort of children. Also, these children do not feature as a defined group in the admissions priorities of schools, unlike looked-after children (who, by law, must be given priority on places).

The same cannot be said of a school that gets a reputation for the quality of its teaching of children with learning difficulties. A statement or EHCP is a lever that can be used, rightly, to secure a place at a school that a parent would like their child to attend, so it can be seen how schools can use this to suggest that they are not particularly good with 'that type of child' and the parent would be better off visiting the school down the road.[2]

Yet, for children with learning difficulties and disabilities in both main-stream and special schools we, as a society, are content for them to struggle to negotiate a steep gradient just to get within shouting distance of the rest of us. Our main achievement for this group has been to build a soul-destroying bureaucracy that drains professionals, infuriates parents and patronises children.

England has a system of support for young people with learning difficulties and disabilities that many would consider to be the envy of the world. I have come across parents who have moved countries, let alone postcodes, to secure a place at an English school for their child. The mother who moved from Moscow to Berkshire so that her daughter could go to school there is but one harrowing example. To be a young child in Moscow, she explained, with autism and currently unable to speak, meant that no education would be provided. It was expected that the child should remain indoors, out of sight and out of mind. The tough, grizzled Muscovite grandfather whom I once had the privilege to show round his granddaughter's school is a man I'll never forget. His daughter interpreted. He cried. I cried. He shook my hand almost constantly and thanked me incessantly. I have heard reports that in Malaysia, parents are paid not to send their children to school if they have learning difficulties; a practice that would not be tolerated in this country.

The Mental Disability Advocacy Centre (MDAC) and the United Nations Partnership on the Rights of Persons with Disabilities released a report in August 2015 on the human rights of persons with intellectual disabilities and/or mental health problems in the Republic of Moldova.[3]

> The biggest barrier however [in Moldova] is stigma, still so palpably felt. We are not yet at the point where the public believes people with disabilities belong – belong in the sense of living and working among us and deciding about their own lives. We do not yet see a society where having a disability is an uninteresting fact, rather than a cause for shame or pity.

Moldova operates a system of guardianship in which people can be deprived of their legal capacity to do things such as get married or sign an employment contract. The process of appointing the guardian may take place without the person with disabilities being present, or they may even be unaware that the process is occurring at all. Guardians can be also appointed without the consent of the person in question, even though the guardian has powers that allow them to place the person with disabilities into a so-called closed institution, against their will, use their allowances and control any assets they may have.

Despite these obvious difficulties it is pleasing to note that the report finds:

> Despite being one of the poorest countries in Europe, the impressive progress made by Moldova in recent years should serve as an important example to its richer neighbours that children with disabilities can study together with other children, and inclusive education is indeed possible and desirable for all.[4]

Human Rights Watch produced a devastating report in 2015 entitled *'Complicit in Exclusion': South Africa's Failure to Guarantee an Inclusive Education for Children with Disabilities*.[5] It detailed how an estimated 500,000 children with disabilities have been shut out of South Africa's education system. Human Rights Watch unearthed the jaw-dropping fact that children with disabilities who attend special schools often have to pay fees that children without disabilities do not. They also found that some parents cannot send their child to school because they cannot pay these fees and the transportation costs of sending their child to school.

We should be proud of our more enlightened and supportive attitude to children with special needs, especially as it has not always been that way. In their 1947 book *Learning and Teaching – an Introduction to Psychology and Education*, A.G. Hughes and E.H. Hughes[6] suggest a basis for dividing children up into 'various types of education'. This can be seen in the table on page 11.

IQ	Type of education	Percentage in the population
50 and below	Ineducable idiots; occupation centres	0.2
50–70	Mentally defective pupils; special schools	2.0
70–85	Dull and backward pupils; special secondary school education	10.0
85–115	Normal pupils; secondary school education	76.0
115–130	Bright pupils; grammar or technical secondary school education	10.0
130–150	Very bright pupils; grammar secondary school education	2.0
150 and above	Exceptional pupils; grammar secondary school education; ultimately university	0.2

It is easy to be shocked by the labels, but this was 1947. I note the neatness of the bell-curve distribution of the percentages, indicating a preference for easy symmetry over the actual number of children who would in 1947 be regarded as exceptional pupils or ineducable idiots, as if the number of ineducable idiots in any society exactly matches the number of children bound for university. Note also that they believe an eye-watering 12% of children require a special school education, compared to today's figure of 1.1%.

I am amused to find that a 1940s version of me would be regarded as normal and destined for a secondary education. I do wonder what occupations would have been open to me in the 1940s, but whatever they were I am sure that an ordinary lad from a secondary school would not have been expected to amount to anything particularly extraordinary. I am sure that the intellectual demands of leading any school, let alone a special school, would have been considered to be beyond a boy such as me. I am thankful that the 1980s and 1990s were kinder.

I am less amused by the label *backward*. My mother informs me that this is precisely the label that was attached to my uncle Thomas in 1950s Ireland. And that is all that Ireland ever did for him. It gave Thomas and my grandparents a label with which to excuse the state's complete lack of interest or sense of responsibility towards him, and left him to it. *Backward* has the stench of counterfeit cologne. It implies someone who's not even facing in the same direction as the rest of society. It's worse than the use of the word *retarded*, along with its counterparts *slow* and *behind*. It's a proxy for a society that has no expectations of that person. Uncle Thomas's learning difficulties were a direct contributor to his traumatic death at the tragically early age of 36. Uncle Thomas's short life is not unusual when it comes to people with special needs:

They die far earlier than the rest of us.

They are far more likely to be bullied at school than the rest of us.

They are far more likely to be excluded from school than the rest of us.

They work far less than us. When they do work, they earn less than we do.

They are far more likely to have mental health problems.

Every single indicator of well-being for a child or adult in this group is dire.

They are marginalised, disenfranchised, rendered invisible and, ultimately, forgotten. Even the things they do achieve count for as close as it is possible to get to zero.

A greater proportion of special schools are judged as Good or Outstanding by Ofsted, England's education inspectorate, compared to mainstream primary and secondary schools. Despite this, Ofsted's annual report for 2014[7] makes no comment on this *at all* in its 42 pages. Indeed, special schools are only mentioned three times, and then only for statistical purposes. Bizarrely they are omitted entirely from the section entitled 'Ensuring that pupils with special educational needs fulfil their potential'. It is inconceivable that Ofsted would somehow manage to omit either mainstream primary or secondary schools from their annual report. It indicates how little thought and respect is afforded this sector. That is a problem.

The percentage of children in Year 6 achieving or exceeding the government's expected standard in their SATs is national news every year. The same is true for the headlines for GCSE and A level. The progress that children with learning difficulties make is never discussed because it is not understood. That is a problem.

The bone-crushing infrastructure the professionals who dedicate their lives to working with children with learning difficulties have to negotiate is a problem.

The cliff edge from which the young adults have to fall after their sixteenth or nineteenth birthday is a problem.

It is a problem that so many parents have to fight tooth and nail to get what the rest of us would consider our children's basic entitlement.

The inability of our political system to let anyone publicly state that anything other than five GCSEs, including English and maths, at a minimum of a grade C is acceptable is a problem.

I have been a teacher for 15 years and have spent ten of those years working in special schools. I have become increasingly frustrated at the lack of interest both in this sector and in children with learning difficulties in mainstream schools. Previously, we had a Prime Minister, David Cameron, who had a son with severe learning difficulties and who attended a special school until his tragic death; an Education Secretary, Michael Gove, whose sister had attended a special school; and a Chief Executive of the National College of Teaching and Leadership, Charlie Taylor, who was the former head teacher of a special school for children with emotional and behavioural difficulties. We could not have been better placed for those with real power and influence to champion this group of young people. Despite this, things have deteriorated. This book describes how the system and those within it, both inadvertently and deliberately, are throwing a cloak of invisibility over this group – and that cloak is getting bigger and heavier.

As soon as we start selecting and judging people instead of welcoming them as they are – with their sometimes hidden beauty, as well as their more frequently visible weaknesses – we are reducing life, not fostering it.

Jean Vanier, *Becoming Human*, p. 23

What am I?

I will die at least 15 years younger than you will.[8]

Long before that, I will be twice as likely to be bullied at primary school as you.[9]

I will be nine times more likely to receive a fixed-term exclusion from school than you.[10]

I will be nine times more likely to receive a permanent exclusion from school than you.[11]

Once I've left school I will be seven times less likely to work than you.[12]

If I am lucky enough to work, it will probably be part-time. It will probably be poorly paid.[13]

I am twice as likely to live in poverty as you.[14]

I am over four times more likely to have mental health problems as a child than you.[15]

I am more likely to have children with their own learning difficulties than you.[16]

I am at least three times more likely to end up in prison than you.[17]

I am a child with learning difficulties.

Notes

1. See *BBC News*, 'Nicky Morgan announces "war on illiteracy and innumeracy"' (1 February 2015). Available at: http://www.bbc.co.uk/news/uk-31079515.
2. See Office of the Children's Commissioner's 2014 report, *'It might be best if you looked elsewhere': an investigation into the schools admission process*. Available at: https://www.childrenscommissioner.gov.uk/sites/default/files/publications/It_might_be_best_if_you_looked_elsewhere.pdf.
3. Mental Disability Advocacy Centre (MDAC) and the United Nations Partnership on the Rights of Persons with Disabilities, *The human rights of people with mental or intellectual impairments in the Republic of Moldova* (2015). Available at: http://www.mdac.org/sites/mdac.info/files/moldova_report_2015_english.pdf, p. 12.
4. Mental Disability Advocacy Centre (MDAC) and the United Nations Partnership on the Rights of Persons with Disabilities, *The human rights of people with mental or intellectual impairments in the Republic of Moldova* (2015). Available at: http://www.mdac.org/sites/mdac.info/files/moldova_report_2015_english.pdf, p. 16.
5. See Human Rights Watch, *'Complicit in Exclusion': South Africa's Failure to Guarantee an Inclusive Education for Children with Disabilities* (2015). Available at: https://www.hrw.org/report/2015/08/18/complicit-exclusion/south-africas-failure-guarantee-inclusive-education-children.http://www.hrw.org/news/2015/08/18/south-africa-education-barriers-children-disabilities.
6. A.G. Hughes and E.H. Hughes, *Learning and Teaching – an Introduction to Psychology and Education* (London: Longmans, Green & Co, 1947).
7. Ofsted, *The Annual Report of Her Majesty's Chief Inspector of Education, Children's Services and Skills 2013/14*. See https://www.gov.uk/government/uploads/system/uploads/attachment_data/file/384699/Ofsted_Annual_Report_201314_HMCI_commentary.pdf.
8. *How People with Learning Disabilities Die* (Glover and Ayub, 2010). Note that this is the best outcome from this study. People with learning difficulties but with no associated condition, such as Down syndrome, die, on average, 15 years earlier than the rest of the population. To have a condition that coexists or is comorbid with a learning disability further reduces life expectancy. People with Down syndrome die, on average, 24 years earlier.
9. *Bullying experiences among disabled children and young people in England: Evidence from two longitudinal studies* (Chatzitheochari, Parsons and Platt, 2014).
10. Department for Education, *Permanent and Fixed Period Exclusions in England: 2013 to 2014* – see https://www.gov.uk/government/collections/statistics-exclusions. Pupils with special educational needs (with and without statements or EHCPs) account for six in ten of all fixed-period exclusions. Pupils with statements of SEN or EHCPs have the highest fixed-period exclusion rate, and are around nine times more likely to receive a fixed-period exclusion than pupils with no SEN.
11. See https://www.gov.uk/government/collections/statistics-exclusions. Pupils with SEN (with and without statements or EHCPs) account for seven in ten of all permanent exclusions. Pupils with SEN without statements or EHCPs have the highest permanent exclusion rate and are around nine times more likely to receive a permanent exclusion than pupils with no SEN.
12. See http://www.ons.gov.uk/ons/rel/lms/labour-market-statistics/july-2015/sty-labour-market-statistics--july-2015.html: this shows that 73.3% of people aged 16–64 were employed in May 2015, compared to Mencap's research (see https://www.mencap.org.uk/get-involved/campaigns/what-we-campaign-about/

employment-and-training), showing that only one in ten people with a learning disability is in work, and this work is often part-time and for low pay.

13. See https://www.mencap.org.uk/get-involved/campaigns/what-we-campaign-about/employment-and-training.

14. The DfE's 2015 census on the characteristics of pupils with SEN shows that in England 28.7% of children eligible for free school meals are identified as having SEN and disabilities, compared to 15.1% of the rest of the school-age population (https://www.gov.uk/government/statistics/special-educational-needs-in-england-january-2015). The Joseph Rowntree Foundation's 2016 report *Special educational needs and their links to poverty* states that in both Wales and Northern Ireland pupils who are eligible for free school meals are twice as likely to have SEN compared to their peers (see https://www.lkmco.org/wp-content/uploads/2016/02/Special-educational-needs-and-their-links-to-poverty.pdf).

15. E. Emerson and C. Hatton, *The mental health of children and adolescents with learning disabilities in Britain* (Lancaster: Lancaster University and Foundation for People with Learning Disabilities, 2007).

16. S. McGaw, *What Works for Parents with Learning Disabilities?* (Barnardo's, 2000).

17. P. Mottram and R. Lancaster, *HMPs Liverpool, Styal and Hindley YOI: Preliminary Results* (Cumbria and Lancashire: NHS Specialised Services Commissioning Team, 2006); P.G. Mottram, *HMP Liverpool, Styal and Hindley Study Report* (Liverpool: University of Liverpool, 2007); Loucks (2007).

Chapter 1

The Apprenticeship of Observation

'How do we have ... run ... schools for children with special needs? How is that working?'[1]

Nicky Morgan, Secretary of State for Education (2015)

'Have you ever visited a special school before?' is one of the first questions I ask all visitors to my school.

We've all been to school. For some of us, that period of our life was a long time ago and much has happened since then. Yet, despite the passage of time, we all have some memories from our school days that will never leave us. If they are anything like mine, they won't be the big set-piece interactions that schools are good at – the prizegiving evening, the sports day, the emotional rollercoaster that is results day in August – they will be the seemingly innocuous, incidental moments that are now all but forgotten to all involved but you. Such is the way memory works. Like a misspelled tattoo, the teachers involved have left an indelible mark on us, for good or ill, that cannot easily be removed. The teacher, for example, who accused me of being a terrorist when she saw me reading a book on the history of the IRA when I was in the sixth form – an action that, carried out today, would likely have seen me labelled as prone to radicalisation and end up the recipient of a visit from the officers of Operation Prevent from the local constabulary.

Yet the best teachers recognise that something that might be regarded as incidental, fleeting or mundane may be life-changing to a student. Chris England, a brilliant teacher of English at Brakenhale School in the 1980s, saw something in me and one day asked me to write for a school magazine he was founding called *Word Up*. He probably does not remember that act yet he alone, by that gesture, and by his teaching more widely, developed in me a love of literature and of writing that has never left me.

What made this event all the more significant was that English was something I feared before I was fortunate enough to cross paths with Mr England in 1986. I feared it because of my class teacher for the last two of my years in primary school. My inability to do well enough to move up from the purple level of the SRA reading scheme, always met with withering frustration by my teacher, resulted in me simply not bringing my work to her any more. For a time this went unnoticed. Or maybe it was simply accepted. Either was fine by me. My memory wants to believe that this lasted for a whole year, but I suspect it was only a matter of a few weeks. Her public humiliation of me when I failed to correctly spell the plurals of *knife*, *hoof*, *thief* and *roof* made it worse. To top it all off, she then reprimanded me in front of the class for wearing a tracksuit to school.

'You look like you're about to play a football match,' she shouted.

I found this baffling, even as an 11-year-old, as our school didn't have a uniform. We were, so I was led to believe, able to wear whatever we liked. Even now, as I write this 30 years later, I can feel my heart rate rising slightly, the knot in my gut returning. Even now, don't ask me to spell the plural of *roof*; I'll need to look it up to make sure.

Perhaps that's one of the reasons I became a secondary school teacher. I didn't particularly enjoy primary school and was in the middle of the class academically. I learned quickly that the ability to do just enough and to keep my head down meant that I could go unnoticed; soldiers call this being the Grey Man – 'Do not get noticed, and do not, under any circumstances, come last' – and I was a half-decent Grey Man. I would have been a better Grey Man had I not had a name that is very distinctive and which few could pronounce. Add to that the fact that some teachers made fun of my name, that I had ginger hair and asymmetric ears, and you won't be surprised to know I was bullied. It was the 1980s. Bullying, as the saying goes, was on the curriculum.

Your memories will be different, but almost all adults think they know how schools work and what it's like to be a teacher because we've all been to school. Dan Lortie calls this 'the apprenticeship of observation'.[2] What this also means is that one of the contributory factors to the invisibility of children with learning difficulties is the fact that so few of us have ever set foot inside a special school. This applies to teachers as much as it does to the general population. Hence my question, 'Have you ever visited a special school before?'

I show parents around the school at least twice a week, and encourage as many other visitors to the school as possible. It is the most effective and simple way of making our school, and the students within it, visible. In at least 90% of cases, the visit is the first a guest has made to a special school. This might sound high, but is unsurprising. A teacher would have to have a very strong reason to take time out of their busy schedule to visit another school, let alone a special school, for anything other than a child protection meeting or a job interview. They're clearly too busy. As a mainstream teacher I was blissfully unaware and completely uninterested in what special schools looked like, who went to them, how or if the curriculum differed from my own school's, and if there was anything I could learn from them. This was, of course, a major mistake. I had at least my fair share of bottom-set groups (it never bothered me back then that we labelled classes as such, yet writing that now reminds me how limiting a label it is), which is where the majority of our students with learning difficulties resided. I look back now and realise how little I knew about their needs and about how to teach them well. I remember relying far too much on teaching assistants to fill in the holes in my teaching, which were gaping. I realise now that some time spent in a special school would have made it abundantly clear to me that my teaching was ill-suited to their needs, and how little I knew about how to assess how well they were doing in my lessons.

I remember that sixth formers in our school raised money every year to take a group of students from Addington School, a local special school, to Tirabad, an outdoor education centre in mid Wales, for a week. The sixth formers would each buddy up with a student from the special school for the week, having got to know them and something about their needs beforehand, and take part in the adventurous activities alongside them. The *Times Educational Supplement (TES)* ran a story on it one year and I recall feeling proud that we were doing such a thing, that it was a noble thing to do, and that the sixth formers would benefit tremendously. Did I seek to find out more? No. Did I endeavour to take part in the trip? No. Did I talk to any of the sixth formers on their return? Not once. That was my sole exposure to special schools, and I considered them a world apart from the mainstream sector. The fact that the overlap between sectors is significant was lost on me. It is no wonder that the vast majority of the workforce in schools has never visited the schools in which the students with the most complex needs are learning.

Perhaps we should all be a bit more like Anne Binding.

Anne Binding was, until recently, co-head teacher of Warfield C of E Primary School in Bracknell in Berkshire, England. Anne got in touch with me a few months back to request a visit to our school. Anne's school is at least 12 miles from my own, in another local authority, and there are three special schools closer to her school than mine, so we have virtually nothing to do with each other. She wanted to visit as she had a student in Year 4 who she thought may be suitable for a school such as ours when the time arrived in Year 7. Anne needed to know what she was talking about so that she could offer some solid advice to the child's parents when discussion around secondary placement arose. Anne's objective for the visit was clear: 'I need to understand what we need to do differently between now and the end of Year 6 so that this student makes the best possible transition.'

I have never had a fellow head teacher say that to me before or since, and I told Anne as much. It was music to my ears and it was a pleasure to show Anne round the school. I didn't need to tell her what to do. Anne was sharp enough to figure it out for herself as she walked around the school talking to the students and the staff, picking up the nuances of how we organised our school, the levels of independence we were expecting, and the personalisation and differentiation required to teach a group of children well, all of whom had complex needs.

I go out of my way to encourage people to come and visit my school. In particular I target SENCos, other senior leaders in schools, trainee teachers, allied professionals such as senior local authority officers, local police officers, and local and national politicians. I'm sure the vast majority of these professionals could identify someone with Down syndrome from the other side of the street. But how many of them have actually talked to someone with Down syndrome? How many have spent any time at all with someone with Down syndrome? How many of them understand what it means to have Down syndrome, or know about the associated health conditions? How many of them understand how a school can best be set up and organised so that children with learning difficulties learn as well as they can? (The Secretary of State at the time of writing clearly has no ideas, as the quote at the top of this chapter reveals.) How many of them understand the cliff edge that the students drop off when leaving school when the support dries up? How many truly know what adult life will be like for these young people? The bald statistics in the introduction section, 'What am I?', should be enough to tell them what adult life is likely to be like, but that hides the emotional stamina required by the young people, their siblings and, most obviously, their parents, just to survive.

I chose Down syndrome, as it is a fairly well-recognised condition among the general public, but the professionals noted above also need to see that there are many and varied reasons why someone may have learning difficulties, and that many of these are hidden. It is not uncommon for visitors to remark to me at some point on a tour of my school: 'I hope you don't mind me asking, but why exactly is that young girl in a special school? I'm not sure what the right word to use is, but she seems ... well ... normal.'

Similar comments come from teachers. A colleague who joined our school recently explained that she expected children to be sitting alone, rocking back and forth quietly. Whatever image you have in your mind of the reality of life in special schools, it is likely to be wide of the mark. This is why the head teachers of special schools and pupil referral units and the leaders of SEN units attached to mainstream schools need to make the first move to bring people in. If we simply sit and bemoan the lack of interest in our sector and hope things will change, then we're in for a long wait.

When I hear comments such as 'They're so engaged in their learning' or 'They're so well behaved,' I wonder what exactly visitors were expecting. In fact, it is argued that such responses reveal an expectation rooted in fear. Jean Vanier, in his exceptional work *Becoming Human*, is clear on this. Vanier has devoted his life to working all over the world with people with, as he calls it, intellectual disabilities. He is right when he states that society shuns weakness and glorifies strength. This results in a fear of those perceived as weak, and that provokes us to exclude and reject others. It indirectly leads us, as a society, to prefer the care of the elderly and infirm, those with dementia or Alzheimer's disease, and adults with learning difficulties in supported living to be conducted out of sight. We can convince ourselves that all is rosy, that these places are havens of serenity and this sanitised view, ultimately, leads to cases such as Winterbourne View,[3] exposed by the BBC's *Panorama*, where adults with learning difficulties were horribly abused and assaulted.

It is this lack of awareness that led me to prejudge many, many children in the earlier years of my teaching career. One particular child remains strong in my memory. Lawrence has Prader–Willi syndrome, which is a condition characterised by learning difficulties and in which the child can show an increased appetite, which can lead to excessive eating and life-threatening obesity. Prior to working with Lawrence, I had never taught anyone with this condition before, but I had seen a programme on Channel 4 about the syndrome and pathetically considered myself well briefed. I went to a colleague for some advice.

> 'Pat, I'm teaching Lawrence this year and I'm worried. My first module is about food and I'm not sure how to manage Lawrence.'
>
> Pat was blunt. 'Have you met Lawrence?'
>
> 'Er, no.'
>
> 'Right. Get to know him, for goodness' sake, and then come back and talk to me in a few weeks if you're still unsure.'

Pat was, as usual, correct. I had made the mistake of predicting failure, one of the features of what the psychologist Dr Aaron Beck calls cognitive distortions, also known as the fortune-teller error.[4] I had predicted trouble, problems and failure in advance of actually being bothered to get to know Lawrence, understand his needs and work from there. It is a mistake, I suggest, that is made up and down the land with depressing regularity.

By maximising the number of people who cross the threshold of my school we can then extend the apprenticeship of observation to its widest possible reach. By maximising the number of people who spend time talking to the students and staff whom I serve, I hope to improve on the number of people who want to be governors as a result of their visits, influence the people who include children with learning difficulties when making policy decisions, persuade more trainee teachers to make the informed decision to work with children with learning difficulties (teacher vacancies are twice that of mainstream schools currently, yet expensive Department for Education (DfE) advertising to entice people into teaching completely fails to mention special schools), and increase the number of teachers who understand that negative behaviour communicates an unmet need.

What can be done to improve the profession's knowledge of special schools?

- Trainee teachers routinely report that insufficient time is given over to SEN on their courses and, as a result, they can feel underprepared to teach such children in mainstream schools and to ensure their needs are well met. (Interestingly, they report feeling the same about behaviour, which leads me to believe that this is a 'kill two birds with one stone' problem.) A compulsory period of time of a meaningful duration spent in a specialist provision – I volunteered to do one of my placements in a young offender institution, only to be told it was only for art teachers – during the course would be a great start. Some university-based courses already do this, but it is less common in school-based initial teacher training. My first ever lesson with a class of Year 10s with severe and profound and multiple learning difficulties made me realise how little I really knew about learning. 'Er … Harry can't talk yet, so why are you asking him to tell you his name?' said a colleague, making little effort to hide her contempt for the fact that I had made such a basic error. I had been a teacher for seven years at this point, but was as helpless as a newborn. Some time spent observing and talking with skilled teachers about how they know if a child with such severe needs has actually learned something should be a career-defining moment. How does a child with a multi-sensory impairment (that is to say, who is both deaf and blind) even know who you are and who else is in the room, let alone what lesson they are in? Has a child *really* learned something if that skill or knowledge can't be repeated the following hour or day or week or month? Has a child *really* learned something if that skill or knowledge can't be transferred to another context, or can't be repeated with another teacher or teaching assistant? Seeing how special schools deal with challenging behaviour would go some way to filling the confidence gap that

trainee teachers report in this area when they take up posts in
mainstream schools.

- All current initial teacher training routes are mainstream-focused.
  If you want to teach in a special school as a newly qualified teacher
  (NQT) you can, but you will arrive with a qualification that has
  been entirely based in mainstream schools or, if you are fortunate,
  you may have had your shorter placement in a specialist provision.
  There are over 380,000 teaching assistants hard at work in
  schools in England, and an increasing number are graduates. This
  is an experienced and skilled workforce who can assist with the
  difficulties many schools are now facing with recruitment. Teaching
  assistants account for a larger proportion of the workforce in special
  schools than in mainstream schools, and many are very highly
  skilled. The DfE needs to make it much easier, both for candidates
  and schools, for people in this group of professionals who wish to
  become qualified teachers to do so. There is a loose analogy with the
  army where it has been standard practice for decades for soldiers
  to be commissioned from the ranks to become officers where they
  show leadership potential. This is considered, rightly and blindingly
  obviously, to be a measure of confidence in the leadership skills of
  British soldiers, who are the envy of armed forces the world over. An
  organisation that grows its own leaders is surely an organisation in
  a rude state of health. The DfE should aspire to a situation where
  teaching assistants are competing fiercely for places on courses to
  become qualified teachers. That would be a strong indicator of
  the improving health of our profession. The current options via
  School Direct are expensive for schools and require a period of
  overstaffing to retain these colleagues on their books while they go
  through training, often in other schools. As budgets bite, this option
  becomes less and less affordable.

- In 2009 it became law for every new Special Educational Needs
  Coordinator (SENCo) in a mainstream school to gain the Master's-
  level National Award for Special Educational Needs Coordinators
  within three years of taking up their post. The DfE could decide
  that the award should follow the lead of the National Professional
  Qualification for Headship (NPQH) and provide a period of
  secondment in another school – in this case, given the nature of the

qualification, they could stipulate that this time must be spent in a special school. I spent a week of my NPQH in a Roman Catholic primary school because, as a secondary-trained special school teacher, these areas (primary schools and religious denomination) were my weakest. It is self-evidently a good thing for SENCos (who are regarded as the fount of all knowledge in their school when it comes to SEN) to broaden their knowledge and experience in this way.

- Ultimately those of us who work in special schools are best placed to remove the cloak of invisibility that covers this sector. We have as much to gain from mainstream schools as they have from us – my own school has an ongoing need to ensure we are doing our best by our most academically able children, and mainstream school colleagues can help us with that. It is incumbent on special school leaders to make it as easy as possible for others to get to know us. There are many simple ways to do this:

  - Offering to be involved in the induction and training of teaching assistants, NQTs and teachers in mainstream schools, and offering placements/secondments as part of that induction.

  - Opening up in-house professional development and training opportunities to mainstream schools. It is highly unlikely that mainstream cousins will offer whole-school training on topics such as fragile X syndrome, pathological demand avoidance syndrome or foetal alcohol syndrome, and may have to resort to expensive external continuing professional development (CPD) for specific students if they find themselves needing such training. Even then, they are likely to offer that training to a small subset of the workforce in their school. Joining up with their local special school would build a bridge and could lead to ongoing support if the school needs it.

  - I notice that work experience is being gradually squeezed into a smaller and smaller corner of the Key Stage 4 (KS4) timetable in mainstream schools. Special schools can offer to assist with placements for students who are interested in learning more about careers with children. We are delighted to host students every year who have ambitions to be teachers or doctors, and are grateful for the opportunity to give young people the chance to learn more about children with learning difficulties.

* Follow Wellington College's lead and build a long-lasting link between students. Students from our sixth form spend part of each week working with students from The Stanley and The Orange boarding houses. Staff in both schools recognise that their students would benefit from spending quality time getting to know others whom they would be very unlikely to meet otherwise. As you can imagine, there is a period of hesitance and reluctance when this partnership renews itself every year with a new cohort of students, but this is soon replaced by a growing confidence and an understanding that the students have more in common than they first thought. Ed Venables, The Stanley's Housemaster, summed it up beautifully when he said, 'When they're together there is no sense of sector; they're simply teenagers.'

Notes

1. See http://schoolsweek.co.uk/
   schools-week-editor-interviews-edcuation-secretary-audio-recording/.
2. D. Lortie, *Schoolteacher: A Sociological Study* (London: Chicago University Press, 1975).
3. See http://www.bbc.co.uk/news/uk-england-bristol-20084254.
4. A.T. Beck, *Cognitive therapies and emotional disorders* (New York: New American Library, 1976).

Chapter 2

Hiding in Plain Sight

'Teachers should have bigger ears and smaller mouths.'

Professor Paul Black

'All negative behaviour communicates an unmet need.'

There's no middle ground with that statement. You either believe it or you don't.

I have had many discussions, some very heated, with teachers, psychologists and other professionals in my time about this and those I've verbally wrestled with seem split 30/70 on this view – and not in my favour. Where there is disagreement, those of us who hold this view are told that we are progressive (in the pejorative sense), that we are free-will deniers, professionally vain and reckless apologists for inexcusable behaviour.

The more vehement opponents of this view tend to underline their argument with something that goes like this:

'Haven't you ever done something just for the sake of it?'

'Like what?'

'Like smashed this cup on the floor.'

A cup is then held at arm's length between thumb and forefinger, eyebrows raised in an I-dare-you-to-dare-me expression.

'No. If you were to do that now, it would be in a futile attempt to win this debate. Your action would indicate that your need to win this argument far outweighed your certain knowledge that to smash that cup would be wrong.'

Checkmate.

The principle that 'All negative behaviour communicates an unmet need' is critically important to me as it has fundamentally changed the way I view the behaviour of children as a teacher. I have presence in the class-room, and that, along with being six foot tall with a booming voice (when I want it to boom), worked for almost all the children I taught in main-stream schools, but was, at the time, mystifyingly ineffective with those children whose behaviour I found most challenging. It has changed me from the novice teacher who was frustrated and who used that voice as a weapon. It has been critical in my ability to lead a school from a position where both the staff and the inspectors judged our students' behaviour to Require Improvement to the point where both the staff and the inspec-tors judged our students' behaviour to be Outstanding. We made that shift within 14 months.

I remain concerned that 'behaviour' and 'special educational needs' are used interchangeably by many educational professionals. This concern arises because of the number of children I see who are having to leave mainstream schools because of their behaviour. At the time of writing, almost 25% of the children in my school have been to a mainstream secondary school and had to leave at some point, almost always due to their behaviour, and my school is not designated as a specialist school for students with social, emotional and behavioural difficulties. Nearly all of these children are boys. They have learning difficulties, sometimes they have associated conditions such as a specific language impairment, dyslexia or autism, but it is their behaviour that results in the placement breaking down. This convinces me that many of us in the profession are not looking anywhere beyond overt behaviour. We see the spots, but we take no time to ascertain if they are a symptom of measles, chickenpox or adolescent acne. As a result we just cross our fingers and hope the spots go away all by themselves.

In his book *Mindware*, the psychologist Richard Nisbett describes the importance of recognising the differences between dispositional and situational factors that affect behaviour:[1]

> [T]here is vastly more going on in our heads than we realise ... Pay more attention to context. This will improve the odds that you'll cor-rectly identify situational factors that are influencing your behavior and that of others ... Realize that situational factors usually influence your behavior and that of others more than they seem to, whereas disposi-tional factors are usually less influential than they seem.

It is a mistake to extend the statement at the beginning of this chapter to mean that children – or anyone, for that matter – cannot be responsible for the choices they make. Of course they are. However, it is a more fundamental mistake to believe that any behaviour, positive or negative, exists in a vacuum, the 'I teach. You behave. You learn' point of view. Context is everything. This view doesn't excuse behaviour; it merely helps to explain it. This became blindingly obvious to me when I worked with children who occasionally presented with some very challenging behaviours. Even the phrase 'very challenging behaviours' needs to be clarified and defined, as it usually conjures up images of confrontational, aggressive and violent boys.

Behaviours that can be regarded as challenging in the context of a school may well be perfectly acceptable – or, indeed, absolutely necessary – outside the classroom. At one end of the continuum they can be challenging when learning is disrupted or, at the other end of the scale of seriousness, the behaviours become self-injurious or injurious towards others. Some of these behaviours will be entirely normal for the child concerned, but are likely to be uncomfortable for you, the other adults and the children in the class to accept. Indeed, some of the behaviours may well be absolutely necessary to the child at that moment, such as sensory-seeking behaviours. These can be a source of frustration for you, as you may want the child simply not to do it. I recall the frustration I felt when I first taught Jonno GCSE science. I distinctly remember asking him politely at the beginning of one lesson to write the date. Moments later I could see at the top of a fresh page in his exercise book the words 'The date please.' He had done exactly as I'd asked, but I was sure that his cheeky smile betrayed some deviousness. It took a colleague who had worked with Jonno as a teaching assistant to educate me that Jonno would carry out my instructions to the letter, so I'd better be explicit with my language. A teacher's frustration is likely to continue if they make no serious attempt to understand the needs that are influencing the behaviour. (Free-willers – note that I didn't say that the need was *forcing* the child to do it.)

Age is a factor here too – teachers in the early years of schooling are well used to children chewing the cuffs of their school sweaters, and it doesn't seem to cause too many problems. The 15-year-old boy with autism who does it all day long, or chews his collar or his own skin instead, can be regarded as a problem. Schools can find it difficult to accept that the young man may benefit from a chewy to satisfy this proprioceptive need, as a teenager chewing a piece of plastic, and the large amounts of saliva that result, may make people feel uncomfortable. An advocate for children with autism, Mark Neary, remarked recently on Twitter, 'Whenever I read something about behaviour intervention for people with autism, the unspoken rule is "let's make them more like us"'.

You can wish as hard as you like for someone with pica to stop eating the graphite inners of your pencils or the plasterboard in the corner of your classroom. You can wish as hard as you like for someone with Down syndrome not to have an enlarged tongue, a heart defect, a hearing impairment or shortened digits, making speaking, listening and writing difficult (and, sometimes, frustrating), or for someone with Prader–Willi syndrome to stop desiring food – but you're in for a long wait. There are many things you can do to improve the situations of all those students, but it takes affirmative action from you and a commitment to understanding the child's needs to begin with.

I have a lifetime's worth of examples that can serve to illustrate how my thinking has ended up at this position, and for which no amount of training or professional development prepared me. The most extreme examples are the most unhelpful. They are the ones that mainstream schools are unlikely to encounter – a child smearing and ingesting their own faeces, a child deliberately banging their head on the side of the swimming pool or on a concrete floor so that they can see their blood dripping into the water and taste it in their mouth, a child masturbating in assembly in the middle of 150 children and 50 staff, a child with an overwhelming desire to ingest batteries. And of course, if mainstream schools do encounter such extreme behaviour, they may well only encounter it once.

Amber

Amber had learned, long before I met her and largely through trial and error, how to secure the attention of adults. Her strategy was remarkably successful. When I first met Amber, I was on duty at lunchtime and she walked straight up to me and, in the sweetest voice imaginable, said 'I love you.' How charming, I thought. Before I could finish this thought she went on to say, 'I love Amy Winehouse.' Interesting one, but children do sometimes take on the musical interests of their parents. In any case, she already had my full and undivided attention.

'Fuck you' immediately followed.

Now, this was unnecessary as Amber already had my full attention and had got me right where she wanted me. However, to Amber this was a successful interaction. She wanted my attention, and it worked. The appropriateness of telling a teacher that they love them, about her musical tastes or the use of language that we don't allow in schools was irrelevant to her. You can immediately see why this is challenging in the context of a school. Teachers do not feel that we can ignore the use of such language, and we don't want other children learning this kind of language. This much is obvious. Look no further than that and you will respond every time to Amber's behaviour. Yet no number of detentions, fixed-term exclusions or time spent outside the head teacher's office was going to change her behaviour. You may well improve it, but it will take you a long time. Or, if it is your view that it is not your role to improve it, perhaps that's when Amber and children like her part company with mainstream schools.

It was going to take the commitment and discipline of all who worked with Amber to resist the urge to respond when Amber used inappropriate language, and to respond very positively when she did not. Responding to it only strengthened the positive feedback loop that Amber sought. In the three years I knew Amber we made significant progress with this, but did not eradicate her desire to secure interaction with adults by swearing. Note that Amber rarely used this language, or any of the stock phrases mentioned above, when talking to other children. They simply didn't respond in the way that Amber had learned that adults do, so she stopped talking to them that way.

George

My wife worked with George following his permanent exclusion from primary school. By Year 5, shockingly, George was using alcohol and marijuana, and eventually he ended up in a secure children's home a couple of hundred miles away. A colleague of my wife's was working with him one day when George demanded, 'Gimme the ruler.' Her colleague uttered the fatal words, 'Say the magic word,' to which she received the response, 'Give me the fucking ruler.' That kind of blatant aggression can be unnerving and infuriating for teachers, but a knowledge of George's life, which my wife and another colleague sought via home visits, pointed towards the gaping holes in his emotional development. Where such holes exist (and they exist for many) they need to be filled by explicit teaching of expected standards of behaviour, coupled with an understanding of how children with emotional regulation issues can, and do, respond to situations they deem as threatening.

Henry

I first met Henry when I was being interviewed for the deputy head teacher's position at Holyport Manor School in Berkshire, England. I remember it distinctly, as it was St Patrick's Day and the canteen had laid on a themed lunch for the students. This proved problematic for Henry as the mashed potato had cabbage in it. To Henry, mashed potato does not look like this. It is plain white and does not have green bits in it. Henry then systematically removed all the green bits, each encased in its own little protective globule of potato, by hand, and threw them onto his tray (and the table) to make the mashed potato look the way it should. The presence of cabbage in mashed potato is so insignificant for almost all of us that we wouldn't give it a second thought (or we would fully understand the reason for its presence). But Henry found society an incredibly stressful place, and it brought his lunchtime to a grinding halt.

This type of behaviour, a genuine attempt by a child to repair that part of the world in front of them that they can clearly see is wrong, can be a source of frustration to the adults working with a child. I reiterate what Mark Neary said: 'Whenever I read something about behaviour intervention for people with autism, the unspoken rule is "let's make them more like us". In this case the obvious solution – giving Henry mashed potato without cabbage in it – would clearly work. However, Henry would also be able to understand that something called colcannon is made from mashed potato and cabbage, and is green and white. It's far better for Henry to spend time preparing him and introducing him to something new than for him to remain within the confines of what we know to be safe.

Dean

I taught Dean when I became a father for the first time, and he taught me how strong the bond is between a child and parent. He had been horribly abused by his mother but would not have a word said against her. He was on a child protection plan and remained living with his mother, around whom his entire world, which was very small indeed, revolved.

He was academically well above average but had been permanently excluded from a mainstream school because of his behaviour, which mainly amounted to the use of abusive language towards adults, and absconding from the school site.

I taught Dean and his classmates to use Bunsen burners so that we could carry out some investigations in chemistry. For almost all the students this was an exciting thing to be doing, and something that was unavailable to some of them in mainstream schools. Dean promptly upped and left at the beginning of one lesson, to be found a short time later at the top of the fire escape in tears. We had developed a very solid relationship and had got to the point where we could always talk things through candidly after an incident. After a significant investment in time (and time spent with children is always an investment), and some deep questioning, this is what I learned:

- Dean was very excited at the thought of using a Bunsen burner;
- Dean really wanted to learn how to use it safely;
- Dean knew he could learn how to do it;
- Dean did not like the feeling that excitement gave him in his belly;

- Dean got the same feeling in his belly when he was scared;

- Dean was unable to tell the difference between the two feelings;

- Dean wanted help to know the difference.

All negative behaviour communicates an unmet need.

To be clear, holding this view is not an underhand way of blaming teachers for the conduct of the students in their class, another common evolution of the discussions I sometimes have with professionals. The inappropriate conduct of a student may well be present with the full knowledge, and in spite of, the rules and expectations in your class or school, and the unmet need may be something you can do absolutely nothing about at that time, but if you retain the position that it is not your role to work that out (take a look at the *Teachers' Standards*, by the way[2]) and that the child should just behave, then working with children with learning difficulties will feel like one long uphill struggle.

I remain baffled by the way that the teaching profession grapples with this. Almost all police officers understand implicitly that negative behaviour is a form of communication that points towards an unmet need, and a failure to understand this would be regarded as a serious gap in the skill set of a constable. How do I know this? Well, that was a topic on which we spent some serious time when I was training to be a Special Constable.[3]

Police officers learn extremely quickly to read the communication behind the behaviour of the members of the public that they are dealing with – and, importantly, their fellow officers with whom they're working – and this is not just reserved for situations that have the potential to become violent. Officers are constantly risk-assessing situations in order to prevent them escalating, to ascertain if someone is telling them the truth, or by reading the body language and other non-verbal cues of those around them. They know that the consequences of getting it wrong can be severe: suspects escape, evidence can be destroyed, the distressed person jumps from the bridge or they, or their colleagues, can be hurt, sometimes fatally. Such consequences, I can assure you, sharpen the senses.

PC Rob Yule of Thames Valley Police, one of the finest officers I have had the privilege of working with, hammered this home to me on my first shift with him with his very first words: 'My aim is to get to retirement without ever having to use this [pointing to his pepper spray], or this [pointing to his baton], by using these [pointing to his ears] and this [pointing to his mouth].'

I could have hugged him.

I contrast that with the sergeant I worked with only once, thank goodness, whose opener was: 'I got rid of my last Special Constable because he didn't like violence enough.' For good measure, he also took the view that everyone was guilty and I just wasn't looking hard enough.

My point is that it is not a sign of weakness to seek to understand the causes of negative behaviour; it is a self-evident professional strength. If you do not fundamentally believe that you can improve the behaviour of a student by your actions (that is, assuming that you actually want to improve the behaviour rather than simply remove it, and the child along with it), then you are likely to remain frustrated at what you see in front of you, as you have rendered yourself powerless.

The excellent 2010 report by Geoff Lindsay and Julie Dockrell, *The relationship between speech, language and communication needs (SLCN) and behavioural, emotional and social difficulties (BESD)*, highlights the complexities of overlapping, coexisting and comorbid needs.

You can label children as naughty and shake your head sadly at what the world has become, or you can consider the kind of evidence detailed below.

> There is now substantial research evidence that children and young people with SLCN are more likely to develop BESD than typically developing young people. Studies have shown prevalence rates as high as 35-50 per cent. However, the relationship between SLCN and BESD is complex. The type of behavioural, emotional and social difficulty is a factor. Indeed, the term itself indicates that it is a generic descriptor for three related but different domains of development. Similarly, there are different profiles of language difficulties. It is also important to consider other factors that might impact on language and on behavioural, emotional and social development, including academic ability (e.g. literacy) and self-concept. Also important are the age of the child and environmental factors, primarily the home and school including the influence of socioeconomic disadvantage.[4]

You can reflect on the way you talk to a child with speech, language and communication difficulties or you can hear yourself saying again and again that they just don't listen. Or you can seek to uncover what's hidden, out of sight, invisible. You can commit to truly understanding that they may well struggle to process the large volumes of verbal communication coming their way. They may have developed the knowledge you are seeking to impart, but are struggling to communicate that to you in the way you want as they have word-retrieval difficulties and are battling with the technical vocabulary of the subject at hand.

I've been in a similar situation myself. A young man joined our school for children with emotional and behavioural difficulties in the middle of the academic year, following a permanent exclusion from a mainstream school. For six weeks, he was one of those children who seems not to listen. Imagine our surprise, then, when we were visited unannounced by the local authority's specialist teacher for children with a hearing impairment:

'I'm here to see Owen.'

'Why?'

'You're not aware that he's deaf in his left ear, then?'

'No, but it explains a lot.'

I had very easily identified that Owen had behavioural difficulties – his presence in our school said as much – but I had left my thinking and efforts to get to know him there. It did not occur to me that there could be a hidden contributory factor.

The behaviour that results from the unmet need is recognised, presumably because it is often what might be described as 'in your face', but the underlying difficulties may be going unseen. I see this regularly in my professional life. Consider the following facts:

> All the students in the school that I serve, bar one, have been to a mainstream primary school.

> Most then move to the school I work in when a special school is deemed a more suitable environment for their secondary education.

> 25% of our students originally went to a secondary school and then left at some point (and not in a good way).

> Almost all of the students transferring are boys.

Almost all of them are leaving secondary schools to come to us because of their behavioural difficulties.

Clearly, these students are not invisible in these schools. They are well known and usually for the wrong reasons, but it is my contention that it is their needs that are invisible. The usual reason cited in a request to change school is that the behaviour of the student is difficult to deal with or has become unmanageable. The underlying driver for the behaviour is often related to communication difficulties coupled with very low levels of literacy of these students, and this is sometimes, but not always, associated with a condition they may have. Time and again I visit students who are unable to read the work in front of them, and/or unable to process the large amounts of verbal information flying their way, and are doing everything in their power to avoid working. Copying, cheating and charming teaching assistants to do it for them are tactics that pay off. Occasionally they will resort to more negative ways to avoid revealing that they cannot read and write as well as everyone else.

I completely failed to understand this when I taught science in mainstream secondary schools. To be fair to the lecturers on my secondary science PGCE, I explicitly remember being made aware of the potential disparity between the reading age required to read the textbooks I would use and the reading age of my students. I was also taught how to assess the reading age level of a textbook or worksheet. Despite this, I didn't do it once.

It is no wonder that I was continually frustrated by Richard in Year 9 and his 'I can't write, I've got a bad hand' routine. I had him down as lazy, rude and lacking in application. I spectacularly failed to realise that he was doing everything he could to avoid writing in order to hide the fact that he could neither spell nor write legibly. He had what I would now estimate to be a reading and spelling age of about seven. It was far more important to him to avoid doing any work that he thought would let the cat out of the bag than to stay out of trouble, and Richard was remarkably successful at this. While practical work was no problem (he had a part-time job in his grandfather's antique shop), no amount of detentions, letters home or periods of isolation would improve his desire to work in my lessons. In fact, he preferred sanctions, because in detentions or periods of isolation we had a lower expectation that he would work, and he knew that teachers would give up chasing missing work after a time. If we looked at what was going on as a challenge for us to win, Richard had to lose. And Richard didn't like losing. Richard 1 – School 0. Looking back, I know that there is much I could – and should – have done. It's hard to see how I could have been more stupid.

Wallflowers and bubbles

'The first principle is that you must not fool yourself and you are the easiest person to fool.'

Richard Feynman (1918–1988), Nobel prize-winning physicist

Statements like 'All negative behaviour communicates an unmet need' are cheap. Anyone can have principles, hold beliefs, make assertions about how they would run a school, or point out how others are getting it wrong. Everyone has the right to their opinions and the right to disagree with others, but philosophical positions are easy to adopt if you can rest easy, safe in the knowledge that the principles you hold will never be tested, will never brush up against reality.

Head teachers have no such luxury. As leaders we obviously hold strong principles, but these are constantly tested by the harsh reality of running an organisation whose effectiveness fundamentally relies on the quality of the relationships between the people involved. Not only do we have to hold on to our own strong beliefs, but we have to convince others to embrace them too. We have to be skilled communicators. If we are unable to articulate a vision that is appealing to our colleagues, the parents, the children and the governors in our schools then we will continue to be frustrated at the inability of our plans to gain any traction while those around us maintain that they have no idea what the school stands for or where it is heading. If those principles do not inform an ethos, a vision and a leadership that results in the children in our schools doing well, then either those principles – or the principal – must change.

By way of an example, I remember with absolute clarity the one and only time I met Dr Chris Tomlinson. Chris was then in his first year as head teacher of Chafford Hundred Campus in Essex and cut a very impressive figure. He was explaining to a small group of Specialist Schools and

Academies Trust (SSAT) developing leaders, of which I was one, how he organised his school – well over 50 option choices for all, mixed year groups classes, heavy personalisation ('If the kids want to learn Japanese, I'll find someone who can teach Japanese'). I was inspired by him and his willingness to stick to what he believed in – even though some thought him dangerously progressive. The same year, Chafford Hundred was placed in a category of concern by Ofsted. Chris admitted that the school had been too ambitious too early, but felt very strongly that he was doing what was right. He made some structural changes but stuck to his core principles. He knew that deep and lasting school improvement takes more than one year. In 2010 Chafford Hundred Campus was the most improved secondary school in the country, and is now rated by Ofsted as Outstanding. Even in the few years that have passed since I first met Chris the accountability climate has changed so significantly that he may well not have had the chance to see his vision through were he to start it in 2016. Like a Premiership football manager losing the first few games of the season, he would have been fired.

As a head teacher myself now, the core principles I stick to have provoked some fascinating discussions with teachers, parents and others with an investment in the education of children. When it comes to the improvement of children's behaviour, some of those people regard my views as permissive, progressive or just plain wrongheaded. In the early days I was told plainly that it would just never work. In fact, some still protest that, even though the evidence proves it does. But the evolution of my beliefs about the improvement of the behaviour of children in schools has been a long and circuitous one. Staff training days didn't change my views, staffroom chats or rows didn't change my views, and neither did school policies. It was only by committing to truly learning about the lives and needs of the children who were viewed as challenging – or, unforgivably, labelled as 'unteachable'[5] – that the truth started to dawn on me. It was only by truly believing that I and my colleagues could really improve things for these children that I started to learn what we needed to do.

Of course, the time before that was easier. It was easier to complain, but not to commit to any meaningful effort to improve things. It was easier to lay the blame at the door of senior managers, principally those with responsibility for standards of behaviour in the school. It was a time characterised by frustration, puzzlement and subversion. For example, it was common practice in my first school for teachers to manipulate the warning system upon which the school's behaviour policy was based. Students received warnings for any conduct deemed to be below our minimum level of expectation. If a student received three warnings, that would result in the issuing of a departmental detention; four warnings resulted in an after-school detention; and five warnings meant that a student was removed from your classroom. Easy. Start some children – you know, *those* ones – on two or three warnings before the lesson starts. It would be the classic fortune-teller error if it weren't for the fact that I had already rigged the tarot cards. My watershed moment? Pursuing a deputy head teacher down a corridor to *demand* that a boy receive a fixed-term exclusion after a situation that I should have handled myself. Pathetic.

A decade of dedicating my professional life to working exclusively with children and young adults with learning difficulties has led me to this point. I see now how the world is a very difficult place for many people with learning difficulties simply to exist, let alone thrive. Since anyone working with young people with learning difficulties must do what they can to improve their chances of being successful once they leave school, this gives our work in special schools, specialist units and the SEN departments of mainstream schools a very sharp focus indeed.

How can we improve the behaviour of our children?

We need to understand that:

- All negative behaviour communicates an unmet need.

- Positive behaviours and expectations need to be explicitly taught and modelled. Waiting for someone to simply 'get it' is futile.

- There will come a time when the supportive structure of the school is no longer there and when this happens the young person must be able to regulate their own conduct and be clear about the boundaries of social norms. A fondness for hugging people, including strangers, for example, is regarded as cute when someone is two. When they are 22, the average person in the street is likely to be far less understanding.

- Sanctions and punishments are largely ineffective for this group of children.

I'm in a minority on this last point, but I cannot think of a single child I've worked with whose behaviour has improved via this method. Children in our school still have to understand and work through the consequences of their actions in the wider sense, but those are times for teachers, teaching assistants or our behaviour support mentor to work with children in a restorative way, with other children if necessary.[6] A journey on the punishment escalator where ever-increasing severity is used to deter children from behaving in a certain way is a waste of energy.

I include both fixed-term and permanent exclusion in this group of ineffectual strategies. Fixed-term exclusion was my sanction of choice if something was serious enough when I first became a head teacher. I used it excessively, and it betrayed weak leadership. I now realise that making the choice to exclude children in the mistaken belief that I would some-how improve the situation was wrong. The logic goes that children, and, by extension, their parents, are shocked into changing by the seriousness of receiving a fixed-term exclusion. I have never seen this tactic succeed in any of the special or mainstream schools I've worked in. Excluding someone for a fixed period as a way of improving the situation is inaction masquerading as action. It makes us feel like we're doing something, when we're doing nothing of the sort. It is respite, not improvement. This was the view of a now former governor who expected to see more fixed-term exclusions as firm evidence of improvement. It would prove how tough we were being on the behaviour of students (no, it wouldn't) and would be a clear deterrent to the other students (again, no).

I can think of one scenario where the use of fixed-term exclusion is sensible, but it has nothing to do with behaviour improvement. When something extreme has occurred, such as when a young child below the age of criminal responsibility brought a knife into a colleague's school and threatened another child, a fixed-term exclusion of a day or two allowed the school to properly assess the situation before deciding on a course of action. If that child was to return to the school, they were clearly duty-bound to have assessed the situation and taken appropriate steps to minimise the risk to all involved. If they couldn't reduce that risk to an acceptable level then they may have had to resort to permanent exclusion.

The question remains. If any sanction or punishment does not improve the child's behaviour or improve the situation, then why would you make the decision to use it? You are simply kicking the can that bit farther down the road.

Sadly, there remains a place for permanent exclusion, but again this cannot be viewed as a method of improving a child's behaviour. It just removes it from your school, along with the child. I have had to resort to permanent exclusion, but only in the most serious of situations. I was badly assaulted once by an 18-year-old student in our reception area. This young man, permanently excluded from another special school and out of education for over a year, had a set of complex needs that meant he experienced a high level of stress and anxiety all the time. My superb colleagues had worked tirelessly for months with him and his mother in order to help him manage his stresses about being at school and about life in general. He made great progress and we were very proud of him, as he was of himself. Despite this, he attacked me and some other colleagues one afternoon for reasons that we were unable to discover. I slept badly that night, wrestling with the determination to keep going with him but knowing deep down that another such incident could put a colleague in hospital. I woke up knowing that he couldn't return. Colleagues were very sad to see him go, knowing that they had made great progress with him over a few months, and I have a profound respect for them for the work they did. Despite that, I knew that I would be negligent as a leader if he remained in school and a colleague was seriously hurt.

This is why some practices that are popular in some charter schools in the USA and are gaining some support from teachers in England concern me. Charter schools are broadly equivalent to academies in England in that they are state schools that are independently run and free of some of the regulations that district schools must adhere to. Annabel Lee, a former teacher at a charter school in New York City, wrote about her experiences in an open letter.[7]

> In any educational environment the first principles to instill in the classroom are respect for self, respect for others and respect for the environment. In this school a 'behavior management system' is in place that

does not support these goals. Children will not succeed in getting into college and in the job market because they respond to authority by being silent and walking in public like robots.

Students are expected to walk in the hallway like robots: silent, hands straight by their sides, a puff of air in their cheeks referred to as 'the bubble' so that they cannot talk, in two straight lines.

No head teacher is against good order, but if lesson changeover times are rowdy, disruptive or dangerous then we need to explicitly teach our children the correct way to conduct themselves when they are with lots of other people, all going about their own business in different directions and at different paces. Walking in corridors in the manner described above is no preparation for adulthood. It is perverse to insist on specific behaviours that do not reflect those of society as a whole, such as 'the bubble' or the 'vertical hand' (an insistence that arms are raised at a very specific angle and in a very specific style), and that nothing else will be accepted. It also smacks of a distinct lack of trust in the children. To insist on highly defined behaviours suggests that the children are incapable of, or cannot be trusted with, learning to do the right thing.

We need our children and young people to leave our school as strong self-advocates. We don't want our children to be wallflowers. They can be vulnerable, and I worry about how open to suggestion many of them are. We need them to be firm, be prepared to say 'no' when they are not content with something, and to have their own beliefs and opinions as well as challenge others on theirs with respect. We don't achieve this by regimented systems such as those described above. It is not the kind of environment that would be conducive to good learning in our school. Besides, all my colleagues would leave.

And so it was that my beliefs came to be tested when I became a head teacher four years ago. I joined a highly successful school that had a string of impressive Ofsted judgements to its name and a strong reputation. Within 13 months the school had moved from a judgement of Outstanding for the behaviour and safety of the students to Requires Improvement. There were two fundamental reasons for this and they were inextricably linked. First, and most importantly, I was unable to convince colleagues quickly enough that our ways of dealing with students whose behaviours were challenging were going to be effective. Second, the effective running of the school in almost every regard had relied too heavily on one person, the previous head teacher, a presence in the school for 37 years, 23 of them as head teacher. There was a real failure in succession planning and this (allied to the fact that we were very different personalities, had very different ways of leading, and held polar opposite views on the promotion, maintenance and improvement of good behaviour) made this a perfect storm.

The behaviour of the students deteriorated fairly swiftly and I struggled, and failed, to ensure that there was good order in the school. There is no abdication of responsibility here – any failure to ensure a safe and positive learning environment rests with me and me alone. The differences between the policies I knew we should adopt and the relationships we should build with the children made the task of getting the school to a position that I was happy with a mammoth one, and I came very close to giving up on it.

Four months into that first year, I decided that I'd had enough. I'd gone from being a perfectly competent deputy head teacher to a novice head teacher, and I became sure that I wasn't up to the job. For the sake of the school, and for my health, I needed to step down. I called our Chair of Governors on a Sunday evening, my wife's birthday, after a stress-filled weekend (I had sat in a restaurant that lunchtime, unable to eat anything as I was sure that I would be sick). I told him that I was resigning. He asked me to think about it for a few days. Weakly, I agreed. I can't remember why. He must have called someone in the local authority, as the area education officer was in my office before 9.30 the following morning. I was having a nosebleed as she walked in and I could see her thinking that I was on the edge of breaking down. That's certainly how I felt.

I stayed. Again, I can't remember why.

Given the length of service of the previous head teacher, and the fact that his wife remained working at the school as a deputy head teacher, I knew that there was likely to be some disruption ahead – the link between the length of service of the previous incumbent and staff turnover is, I believe, generally accepted. However, two things happened on the very first day of the academic year that made me change things far more quickly than I had anticipated.

Before school on that first morning a colleague entered my office and handed me an A4 piece of paper: 'Here's the rota for Year 10 to clean the staffroom.' It was a short conversation. My response was to say that no school of which I was the head teacher would have children cleaning the staffroom. If we couldn't be bothered to keep it clean ourselves then it would remain dirty. Of course, this immediately upset my colleague, who retorted that Year 10 have always cleaned the staffroom! I was acutely aware that such swift action would unsettle colleagues, but it was a not-in-my-name moment. The rota went in the bin.

At the end of that day I was asked if I was going to dismiss the children. I looked quizzically at my colleague, who led me into the main hall where the children, some well over six feet tall and aged 16, were sitting on the floor in rows, waiting to be dismissed. Again, that practice was swiftly ended. You can see how the removal of all that upheld a previously successful system led to problems. I was asked by a governor at the time if I could start off like the previous head teacher and then slowly move to my own preferred style of management. An even shorter conversation ensued. My answer was no.

We addressed our collective tendency towards what the psychologist Aaron Beck called 'cognitive distortion' – focusing on negatives, ignoring positives and predicting failure (the fortune-teller error I mentioned earlier). We worked at building great relationships with the students, supporting colleagues when things didn't go so well, and ensuring that the behaviour policy didn't require the presence of one person to hold it all together. We expected the students to talk to, and respond to, all members of staff in exactly the same way. We improved the confidence of colleagues who didn't initially believe they were able to improve the behaviour of students. We regretfully said farewell to colleagues who fundamentally disagreed with our approach. We recruited colleagues who truly believed in what we were trying to achieve. We gathered as much information as we could, initially in a very cumbersome way but then, later, in a much improved manner, and shared it as widely as possible to bolster confidence and to counter any doubts.

Ofsted came back 14 months after their initial inspection and agreed with us that behaviour was now Outstanding. Not perfect, you understand. There's always room for improvement.

I remind myself of that two-and-a-half-year period when I hear assertions that my beliefs and those of my colleagues just wouldn't work in the real world. My principles were tested and survived that brush with reality intact, and are now much stronger for it.

What could be done to improve the teaching profession's knowledge and understanding of the underlying needs that may influence the behavioural issues children with special needs may present?

- It is encouraging that DfE has acknowledged that student teachers need more training on behaviour, and it has set up a working group to do this important work. It is unclear whether the group will advise specifically on children with SEN, but I would regard it as an omission if teachers entered the profession without some understanding in this area.

- If this is done well, then teachers should be prepared to appreciate any differences there may be in the chronological, emotional and cognitive maturity of their children with learning difficulties (this is sometimes called a 'spiky' profile as the relative strengths of different areas would, if plotted on some form of graph, map out a line characterised by peaks and troughs). An approach can then be taken that acknowledges that we need to explicitly teach children the desired behaviours they have yet to learn to consistently manage independently. We completely accept this with gaps in the acquisition of academic skills. If a child is struggling to learn to read, we don't persist with strategies that are not bearing fruit, but we do amend our approaches to try to improve the situation. We don't simply expect the child to 'get' reading, yet we can allow ourselves to be frustrated when children haven't yet acquired the skills to regulate their own behaviour in line with the majority of children their own age, and we make less effort to understand the underlying needs that are driving this.

- Seek the advice of other education and health professionals who bring a fresh perspective. It is likely that mainstream colleagues have come across an educational psychologist in their class from time to time – primary colleagues more than secondary, given that most children who are assessed for EHCPs (or 'statements', as was) are in that age group – and they can be incredibly useful in helping to understand the unmet and often unseen needs that influence challenging behaviours. It was therapists, though, who really revolutionised my understanding of behaviour. As a mainstream teacher I never met a therapist, didn't understand what they did, and would have struggled to see how medical professionals could help me with my teaching. I can see now that I would have developed a far more rounded view of the development of a child (more of that below with regard to psychotherapists) and been far more creative with my approaches to improving behaviour had I spent time with colleagues from these fields.

- Speech and language therapists (SALTs) – it was a revelation to me that the role of SALTs extends to more than working on the diction of children who have delays in the acquisition of speech. SALTs educated me in the broader difficulties that children can have with the development of speech and language skills such as word retrieval (the child wants to say 'caterpillar', for example, but can't retrieve the word, so there are ways to help the child retrieve the word 'caterpillar' by asking them to describe what it looks like, its size, where you might find it, etc.), listening skills ('receptive language' in the jargon), and sequencing of instructions (very useful in lessons such as science when doing experiments, or in cooking lessons with recipes), to name but a few. The understanding of the frustrations that can arise for children with difficulties in some or all of these areas went an awfully long way to helping me appreciate the link between speech, language and communication needs and social, emotional and behavioural difficulties (as noted by Lindsay and Dockrell, 2010).

- Occupational therapists (OTs) – before working in special schools I thought that OTs worked with people who had acquired brain injuries or had a stroke and required some rehabilitation in order to regain lost skills. I had no idea that they are experts at understanding a person's daily tasks (known as 'occupations', hence their name) and then identifying the difficulties they face with those occupations.

Having OTs spend time in my lessons and then suggesting alternative ways of doing things, or the use of specific equipment or adaptations, made me realise how crucial it was for me not to disadvantage any further the children who had problems with fine and gross motor skills. I did not appreciate all the factors that led to good handwriting, for example, and all the things I could do to support this (ensuring good posture, providing a pencil grip, a foot stool or a writing slope). The range of simple equipment such as scissors, chopping boards with integrated knives, specially shaped pens and pencils or ergonomic seating that can support everyday classroom activities (and, crucially, maintain independence for some children) is unknown to many. School uniforms with their zips, buttons and labels can slow down the acquisition of personal care skills such as changing for PE and independent toileting, so it is a clear advantage for all children to maintain their dignity and independence in this area, and OT advice is the best means to achieve this. The frustrations and subsequent challenging behaviours that may arise from struggling with these tasks can then be avoided and independence maintained. If you don't believe me, try doing a jigsaw while wearing boxing gloves. That's what it feels like!

The most important area that OTs can provide expertise in, though, when it comes to managing children's behavioural challenges, relates to 'sensory integration', especially for children with a sensory processing disorder. Sensory integration refers to the way the nervous system receives messages from the senses and turns them into appropriate motor and behavioural responses. We are all doing this constantly with no conscious effort, but it causes problems for those who are hyper or hyposensitive compared to their peers. Precisely because we do this with no conscious effort, it remains an invisible difficulty for many children, and one that is often misunderstood. For *hypersensitive* children, this can manifest itself in a difficulty with the sensation caused by labels or buttons, differences in temperature, strong smells, tastes or loud noises. *Hyposensitive* children may seek out sensory stimulation as they feel understimulated (the child mentioned above ingesting their own faeces is an extreme example). Teachers are more likely to encounter children who may just be very loud, appear intransigent about taking their jumper off in very hot weather, or who have a very high pain threshold. OT advice about how to appropriately substitute that sensory difficulty (it won't go away, so it needs to be substituted with something – when the original behaviour is something such as eating faeces, the motivation to change this is high) can make the life of all involved that much better. I remember being shocked when I first saw a child riding down the corridor of a special school on a scooter. Now I no longer raise my eyebrows, but fully understand that a child going to their next lesson on a bouncy hopper or leaping on a trampoline is part of a carefully planned OT programme and I appreciate the necessity of just such an approach.

- Child and adolescent psychotherapists – I have worked with and learned from psychotherapists when I've taught children who have experienced trauma (parental abuse, in all the cases I've dealt with) in earlier life, sometimes as babies or toddlers, and this trauma has manifested itself in behavioural and emotional problems later on. I remain fascinated that the effects of such abuse can have such a powerful and persistent impact years later, even though the children cannot always remember some of the acts, due to their age when they occurred. Therapists carefully observe children and respond to what they might be communicating through their behaviour and play. This is where I arrived at my belief that negative behaviour communicates an unmet need. Psychotherapists were able to teach me a lot about child development, a subject about which I knew nothing before I became a parent, as it did not feature in my training as a teacher of secondary-aged children. Psychotherapists can explain how developmental gaps in earlier life create cognitive and emotional difficulties later, and can make suggestions for what can be done to help. I see a growing need for access to child and adolescent psychotherapy services in the coming years, as concern grows about the high levels of mental health difficulties in our young people.

Notes

1. R. Nisbett, *Mindware: Tools for Smart Thinking* (London: Penguin, 2015), pp. 48–49.
2. Department for Education, *Teachers' Standards* (2011). Available at: https://www.gov.uk/government/publications/teachers-standards.
3. Special Constables, not to be confused with Police Community Support Officers, are warranted officers who have the same powers, uniform and equipment as regular PCs and their uniform is almost indistinguishable.
4. G. Lindsay and J. Dockrell, *The relationship between speech, language and communication needs (SLCN) and behavioural, emotional and social difficulties (BESD)*. Department for Education Research Report DFE-RR247-BCRP6, 2010. Available at: https://www.gov.uk/government/uploads/system/uploads/attachment_data/file/219632/DFE-RR247-BCRP6.pdf, p. 9.
5. 'Anyone below grade C, Jarlath, is Un. Teach. Able. Fact.' As a colleague once said to me.
6. When I say 'consequences', I mean that in the wider sense, as opposed to simply the consequences to the child. Joe Bower, a teacher from Alberta in Canada, writes very persuasively on that on his blog, see http://www.joebower.org/2010/10/consequences-for-whom.html.
7. See http://dianeravitch.net/2014/03/27/confessions-of-a-teacher-in-a-no-excuses-charter-school/.

Chapter 3

Don't Send Him in Tomorrow

'The students who require the most love are the ones who will ask for it the most unloving of ways.'

Lynne Frost, former Principal, David Young Community Academy, Leeds

The section titled 'What am I?' in the introduction provides you with the stark facts about the increased chances of children with special educational needs being excluded from school. The Department for Education's report *Permanent and Fixed Period Exclusions in England: 2013 to 2014* found that a child with special educational needs is up to nine times more likely to receive a fixed-term exclusion than a child without such needs. Based on my experiences of the past ten years, I suspect this is an underestimate. I have seen, both in schools that I have worked in and schools that I have visited, the use of unofficial or illegal exclusions of children with SEN. Maybe children without SEN get treated in the same way. If they do, I haven't seen it, although maybe I'm less likely to find such evidence, given my position.

Allegations of the use of such exclusions occasionally make the national press – when, for example, a parent goes public to allege that their child has been asked to stay at home for the duration of an Ofsted inspection, such as the case that was reported by the *Daily Telegraph* in February 2015 of a school in Wiltshire.[1] The school was previously judged to Require Improvement in February 2013, when it was 'told to do more to help children with extra needs'. In an incredible statement, a governor of the school commented that:

Two types of students have been involved in this, one of which was those who are very autistic children whose parents or carers were contacted by the school because of the Ofsted visit and because of the change in routine they would be kept at the Link Centre [a support unit for special needs children]. The second group were children who had a history of being disruptive in class, that's my understanding. I'm very sure that no staff would try to tell children to stay at home. There was a very small handful where some people with a track record of causing disruption were taken out of class because you don't know what they are going to do. My belief is the school did what was in the best interest of the whole school and their objective is to get a good Ofsted report.

A spokesman for the school later said interestingly that 'the views expressed by the governor were neither authorised or endorsed by the Board of Governors of the school.'

I have yet to encounter personally the use of unlawful exclusions during the course of an Ofsted inspection to hide from an inspection team something that the school leadership is clearly embarrassed about, but one parent I interviewed for this book reported something that sails very close to the wind: 'When Ofsted were due to arrive I was asked if Sally could visit possible secondary schools, or if she was tired to keep her off. When picking her up her teaching assistant stated that she was asked to take Sally out of the classroom and for a walk and play outside to get her out of the way!'

I have seen on numerous occasions the use of illegal exclusions in a planned way to limit the time a particular student spends in school. For example, when visiting a student in their primary school I was told that I could only visit between 9am and 11am as Sheridan would not be in at any other time. When I arrived at the school, I spent some time with the SENCo. I asked about the restricted timetable.

'Sheridan goes home at 11am each day because he becomes unmanageable by that time,' she said.

'So, how many fixed-term exclusions has Sheridan had this term?'

'Er, none. Why do you ask?'

'When a child is sent home during the day as a result of their behaviour, that is a fixed-term exclusion,' I explained.

'You'll need to talk to the head teacher about that. Look, we're an academic school. We're not set up to deal with this sort of thing.'

I didn't have the heart to pursue it any further with them. I can forgive a SENCo for not knowing the law regarding the exclusion of children from a school, but I find it very hard to believe there is a head teacher out there who is unaware of sections 12 and 13 of the DfE's *Exclusion from maintained schools, Academies and pupil referral units in England*:[2]

> 12. It is unlawful to exclude or to increase the severity of an exclusion for a non-disciplinary reason. For example, it would be unlawful to exclude a pupil simply because they have additional needs or a disability that the school feels it is unable to meet, or for a reason such as: academic attainment/ability; the action of a pupil's parents; or the failure of a pupil to meet specific conditions before they are reinstated. Pupils who repeatedly disobey their teachers' academic instructions could, however, be subject to exclusion.
>
> 13. 'Informal' or 'unofficial' exclusions, such as sending pupils home 'to cool off', are unlawful, regardless of whether they occur with the agreement of parents or carers. Any exclusion of a pupil, even for short periods of time, must be formally recorded.

No one can know with certainty that a child's conduct will deteriorate by a precise time or if it will deteriorate at all. It is the definition of the classic fortune-teller error: that is to say, the prediction of failure. (I also wanted to know what an 'academic' school was. Parents report to me that they hear this term used a lot when they are touring potential schools for their child.) In this case it was simply used to limit the amount of time Sheridan spent in the school. He went home at 11am even if he had a flawless morning, something which is clearly unforgivable.

I never did get to see the head teacher, but I would have been keen to ask how the school was using the money it received from the local authority for the rest of the 32.5 hours a week of support that Sheridan was entitled to from a teaching assistant. When I returned to my school, however, I let the local authority know what was happening to Sheridan, as his parents had a niggling suspicion that something wrong was being done to their child. My actions were in vain, as it turned out – the LA did nothing.

Legislation also mandates that a head teacher must report termly to their governing body about the level of exclusions at the school.[3]

> 38. The head teacher must, without delay, notify the governing body and the local authority of:
>
> • a permanent exclusion (including where a fixed period exclusion is made permanent);
>
> • exclusions which would result in the pupil being excluded for more than five school days (or more than ten lunchtimes) in a term; and

- exclusions which would result in the pupil missing a public examination or national curriculum test.

39. For all other exclusions the head teacher must notify the local authority and governing body once a term.

This is a critical piece of information for a governing body as a basic indicator of behaviour in their school that can be considered alongside the other information they should have about the conduct of the children in the school. If they do not have this information, then how are they to reasonably challenge the head teacher on the judgements he or she makes about the quality of student behaviour in the school? The issue remains invisible, and it is difficult for the governing body to support the head teacher if they are not in full possession of the facts. I mention this as, historically, information about exclusions was not provided to the governing body of my school. In the year before my arrival we recorded 320 sessions of fixed-term exclusion in a school of 120 pupils. Given that number, which I would suggest is on the high side, it would have been crucial to challenge the leadership of the school on why so many exclusions were considered necessary. If they were deemed necessary, it would then allow the governing body to explore with the leadership team if the use of exclusion had been effective in improving the behaviour of the children concerned.

What possible reasons could a head teacher have for choosing to not formally record a fixed-term exclusion? I have already dismissed the notion that the head teacher may be unaware of the legislation on exclusion. This would be a clear competency matter. I consider there to be three main reasons:

- In the example detailed above, the head teacher would have had to write to the parents every day, copying in the local authority's exclusions officer, to explain the reason(s) for the fixed-term exclusion. The local authority would start to make enquiries before too long and, on a day when Sheridan displayed impeccable behaviour, the letter would have to be a work of fiction.

- The head teacher is aware that repeated use of fixed-term exclusion means that the school will come up against the annual limit of 45 days of fixed-term exclusions for any child. Once this happens, the tactic has run out of road. Illegal exclusions are obviously not counted so, in Sheridan's case, the tactic of shortened days would have self-destructed in 90 days if all those missed afternoons had been properly recorded as an exclusion. Additionally, the exclusions would end up on the child's record, and this may be seen as a barrier in persuading another school to take the child.

- The head teacher is concerned that the governors and/or Ofsted (the latter, more likely) will be concerned that the number of fixed-term exclusions points to an issue with behaviour in the school. I know that Ofsted do not automatically take this view, but a number that may seem high should feature in questions from governors and should be scrutinised by an inspection team.

In the above scenarios, the use of illegal exclusions to improve behaviour is an illusion: paralysis dressed up as action. I am reminded of the apocryphal tale we were told as Special Constables in training about two police officers who kicked the severed head of a murder victim down the road into the neighbouring constabulary's jurisdiction so that it became someone else's problem.

If a head teacher truly believes that the use of exclusion is necessary, then they should make that decision and follow the process, just as the law allows and, indeed, demands: summon up the moral courage to put their name on their headed notepaper, write the letter, and be prepared to fight their corner if (or when) questions arise from Ofsted, the local authority or the school's governing body.

The Office of the Children's Commissioner has researched and reported on this matter in the first document that provides quantitative evidence from teachers and school leaders about the scale and nature of illegal exclusions from schools in England. Titled *Always Someone Else's Problem*, it is hard-hitting and uncompromising, and makes uncomfortable reading for many. As unsurprising, depressing and predictable as a bank holiday downpour, they note that '[t]his illegal activity appears to impact disproportionately on those groups which are also most likely to be formally excluded, particularly children with SEN.'[4]

In the context of our group of children, the most worrying finding of the lot has nothing to do with behaviour that has become unmanageable; it is the finding on page 7 of the same report that '2.7 per cent of schools have sent children with statements of SEN home when their carer, classroom support or teaching assistant is unavailable. If these were evenly spread across the country, it would represent 650 schools, or an average of more than four schools in every local authority.' This is worrying for a host of reasons. On the face of it, this would seem to represent an attitude of ownership over the child – 'their' teaching assistant is not present. I have encountered this before when training teaching assistants. I once asked a group to talk to me about where they worked, the year group and/or subject(s) they worked with, and such like. The first three colleagues all began with 'My statement is/has…'. I suspect the second and third colleagues had simply carried on in the same vein as the first, but I called a halt.

'First, they presumably have a name? Second, a statement of SEN is not their sole or defining characteristic or achievement. Third, they're not yours.'

Let's be generous and assume that in some cases there could be a compelling medical reason for being sent home simply because a member of staff is absent. The child has an insulin pump, a vagus nerve stimulator, is tube-fed, or has a tracheotomy that requires specific training in order to operate it. It is easy to see how a complete absence of trained staff in the school could lead to problems.

Our school welcomed a young man last year who had recently had an insulin pump fitted to manage his diabetes better, alongside his other complex medical and learning needs. A number of staff spent the afternoon of our first training day back after the summer break with a specialist diabetes nurse being trained to use the insulin pump and its hand-held communication device. Initially the nurse was very reluctant to conduct the training with what she considered to be an excessively large number of people. We informed her that the nature of a secondary special school (where the student would have many more teachers than in a primary school, and the nature of activities, such as trips and visits off-site and swimming) meant the need to have a fair number of staff trained. She finally agreed.

For good measure, the child's mother attended too, which was incredibly helpful to us, but also helped reassure her that we knew what we were doing. She was able to see that we understood her son's needs in their entirety, and it also brought us a welcome vote of confidence from her.

The nurse's reluctance stemmed from two concerns. First, she was worried that too many staff meant that some of us wouldn't carry out the tests often enough, would become rusty and make a mistake. This is a very good point and a perfectly legitimate one. I am one of the trained staff and someone in the office will regularly tell me that I haven't tested this child's blood sugars for a while so now it's my turn. Quite right, too. Second, the nurse said it was usual for one member of the office team or one teaching assistant to receive the training. Therein lies the problem. If there are children left unsupported due to medical conditions in school who are then forced to go home, it is down to poor foresight and planning from the school.

The charity Contact a Family carried out a survey in 2012 and 2013 with parents to establish how often illegal exclusions happen and to ascertain the impact on families.[5] The results, which I've summed up here, are even more shocking than the Children's Commissioner's report:

70% of those reporting an illegal exclusion had a child with a Statement of Special Educational Needs.

Some of the reasons given for illegally excluding the children were:

- not enough staff to support the child;
- an activity or trip wasn't suitable for their child;
- the child needed to 'cool off' after an incident;
- the child was having a bad day.

The survey provides some strong evidence on the effect of such actions on families, noting that:

- a large minority were having to take a lot of time off work, with even more unable to work at all;
- a majority reporting that it caused conflict with their child's teachers;
- hearteningly a majority felt able to challenge schools, but this often resulted in no improvement in the situation.

Sadly, the report notes that, 'Changing schools is often the final outcome' (p. 3).

The other factors that can influence head teacher behaviour in the practice of illegal exclusion are clearly the potential incentives, such as the absence of that child from the school site for the duration of an Ofsted inspection or the likelihood of not getting caught and the near certain absence of a subsequent sanction.

The biggest factor, though, in my view, is parents not knowing this is illegal. Sheridan's parents, both very well educated, were unaware that he was being treated illegally. Page 7 of the Children's Commissioner's report explains why: 'In our evidence-gathering, the impression from parents and young people was that in dealing with these symbols of authority, they trusted schools and head teachers to act reasonably, in good faith and within the law. They were generally reluctant to challenge schools' authority to act.'

We have to do better than this. The use of illegal exclusion is clearly an issue of misconduct, and mechanisms already exist to deal with this kind of behaviour. It is time that we used them and put to an end this discriminatory practice.

So what can be done to prevent schools unlawfully excluding children?

- Schools should consider the training implications for staff if a particular technique or skill is required to support a child with a specific need. The balance between having sufficient staff available in order to avoid the inability to manage that need, should any of those trained staff be absent, needs to be weighed against the need to keep competency levels high through regular practice. This is less complicated than it sounds, and rests on good communication between the medical professionals, school staff and parents, and the child if appropriate. This can prevent schools finding themselves saying to parents that they must accompany their child on a trip or a residential activity as no trained member of staff is available.

- It is regrettably not unheard of, but thankfully very rare, to learn of head teachers who have faced disciplinary action for tampering with SATs papers or for financial impropriety, but I cannot find a single example of action being taken against those who unlawfully exclude children. There must be a realistic prospect of head teachers being held to account when they make such serious decisions. Given that there is an accepted, lawful mechanism by which a head teacher can exclude a child, any use of unlawful means must be regarded as a deliberate decision to circumvent that process. However, even for lawful exclusions, independent review panels have no power to reinstate pupils – despite their power to quash the decision of a governing body to exclude.

- The extract from the Children's Commissioner's report cited above 'they trusted schools and head teachers to act reasonably, in good faith and within the law' is telling. Parents need to understand the law with regard to exclusion. Given that I am referring specifically to children with SEN, there are opportunities along the way to inform parents of the law in this matter. For those with children with EHCPs, the information can be included as part of the formal paperwork process when an EHCP is completed. I am fully aware, though, that parents can feel inundated with information and paper at times like this, so this piece of information could easily go unnoticed. For those with children without EHCPs it would be incumbent upon the schools to do this – when, for example, the child is given SEN support at the school.

Notes

1. D. Barrett, 'Disruptive pupils "hidden" by school during Ofsted visit', *The Telegraph* (13 February 2015). Available at: http://www.telegraph.co.uk/education/11411290/Disruptive-pupils-hidden-by-school-during-Ofsted-visit.html.
2. Department for Education, *Exclusion from maintained schools, Academies and pupil referral units in England: A guide for those with legal responsibilities in relation to exclusion* (2012). Available at: https://www.gov.uk/government/uploads/system/uploads/attachment_data/file/269681/Exclusion_from_maintained_schools__academies_and_pupil_referral_units.pdf, p. 6.
3. Department for Education, *Exclusion from maintained schools*, p. 10.
4. Office of the Children's Commissioner, *'Always Someone Else's Problem': Office of the Children's Commissioner's Report on illegal exclusions* (London: Office of the Children's Commissioner, 2013). Available at: http://www.childrenscommissioner.gov.uk/sites/default/files/publications/Always_Someone_Elses_Problem.pdf, p. 6.
5. Contact a Family, *Falling through the net. Illegal exclusions, the experiences of families with disabled children in England and Wales (2013)*. Available at: http://www.cafamily.org.uk/media/639982/falling_through_the_net_-_illegal_exclusions_report_2013_web.pdf, p. 3.

Chapter 4

World Beaters

'One principle stands out. Those who work in these schools aim never to give up on a child.'

Dr Christine Gilbert,
former Her Majesty's Chief Inspector of Schools, 'Twelve Outstanding
Special Schools: Excelling through inclusion' (2009: 2)

Each year Ofsted publishes its annual report into its view on the state of the education offered to children in our schools. The 2013/14 report[1] made interesting reading. It pointed out that primary education was improving, and that this was due to the rapidly improving state of leadership in primary schools, but that progress in secondary schools had stalled, again citing leadership as a cause for this. It highlighted that children from poorer backgrounds were still too far behind other pupils. In a measured tone that is often absent from the discussions around free schools and academies, it found that it was too early to judge the overall performance of free schools. It contained a number of informative case studies.

It included a section entitled 'What does the sector look like?' which detailed the proportions of primary and secondary schools that were maintained by local authorities, those that were academies and those that were free schools. These proportions for nurseries, special schools (similar to primary schools, if you're interested) and pupil referral units were, it seems, not worth discussing. There was a similar graphic for the most recent overall effectiveness judgements for primary schools, secondary schools and, interestingly, free schools (despite the fact that there are four times more special schools than free schools). Again, the most recent inspection judgements for special schools were not noteworthy.

You will not learn a great deal about children with learning difficulties and SEN from this report. You will learn the bare statistics about the inspection outcomes of special schools alongside the other school sectors, including nurseries (which have the best inspection outcomes of all school sectors), but nothing else. Any questions you may have about why nurseries and special schools seem to be performing at a high level will remain unanswered.

So what?

Here are the inspection judgements for all schools in England up to March 2016:[2]

Type of school	Number inspected	Percentage of inspections				% Good or better
		Outstanding	Good	Requires improvement	Inadequate	
Nursery	406	60	39	1	0	99
Primary	16,169	18	68	13	1	86
Secondary	3,146	22	54	20	4	76
Special	1,004	38	54	6	2	92
Pupil referral unit	322	18	66	11	4	84
TOTAL	21,047	21	65	13	1	86

Over half of all nurseries and over a third of all special schools in England are judged by the government's inspectorate to be Outstanding. Over 90% of all special schools and almost all nurseries are judged to be at least Good. This is spectacular, and would be front-page news if it applied to either primary schools or secondary schools. Note also that pupil referral units – in my view, this country's poor, illegitimate cousin in the education family, with all of the associated issues that come with a transient population who have social, emotional and behavioural difficulties – also have a better profile than secondaries.

Before we go any further, I need to make it clear that all of these different types of school are inspected using exactly the same framework.[3] This is often news to colleagues, and I've had a wide range of comments before, such as:

'I didn't think that special schools were inspected.'

We are.

'They [Ofsted] don't take into account progress with you, though, do they?'

They do.

'Inspectors don't really know what they're looking at when they visit your school.'

In my experience, they clearly do.

I also need to make it clear that special schools and pupil referral units are, on the whole, inspected more frequently than mainstream schools. The law allows mainstream schools that are currently holding an Outstanding judgement from Ofsted (which may be a few years old) to be free from routine inspection, subject to a remote, periodic risk assessment. There is no such provision for special schools and pupil referral units that are judged to be Outstanding. They are inspected with the same frequency as mainstream schools that are judged to be Good. They, and the students within, may well be effectively invisible when it comes to Ofsted's annual report, but they are very much in the spotlight, if not the limelight, when it comes to inspection. I have a colleague who is the head teacher of an infant school that was last inspected eight years ago. I have been a head teacher for just over four years and have had three inspections in that time (and we are awaiting our next one within the next academic year), and seven in the past ten years as a senior leader.

Given the remarkable success that special schools (and, lest we forget, nurseries and pupil referral units) have achieved, as indicated by Ofsted's inspection outcomes (the only external judgement of quality that we, the taxpayer, and the parents have open to us), why isn't this headline news?

Why isn't Her Majesty's Chief Inspector of Schools lauding the success of special schools and pupil referral units and challenging our mainstream cousins to do the same? Given the spotlight that HMCI is under, you would think that he would take every opportunity to praise a sector that could reflect well on their own organisation. Maybe it's because the risks of doing so far outweigh the benefits to HMCI, and to Ofsted.

First, there hasn't been a spectacular rise in the number or proportion of Good and Outstanding judgements in recent years for special schools and pupil referral units, so no amount of raising the bar can be attributed to improving these schools. Second, there's a risk that highlighting some of the features that make special schools and pupil referral units successful (small, highly personalised, highly flexible and responsive staff with a deep understanding of child development) are unreproducible, or are prohibitively expensive, especially for secondary schools.

Why isn't the Secretary of State for Education seeking to work out just what is happening in special schools that may not be happening in the mainstream sector? The point about some of the features of successful special schools and pupil referral units also applies here.

Factor in the noises that employers' organisations, principally the Confederation of British Industry (CBI), make on a regular basis, usually around exam results time in August, about their dissatisfaction with the quality of school leavers. Children in these schools are not included in the mix when the CBI bemoan (but abdicate complete responsibility for) the ability of some young people to arrive in the job market, work-ready.

A number of questions, concerns and insecurities about their own knowledge of these sectors may remain in the minds of those in positions of power, and I contend that they all contribute, in varying degrees, to the current deafening silence on the relative success of special schools when judged against the Ofsted inspection framework.

It is likely that senior policy-makers and those in positions of influence and power, including special advisers and senior civil servants, as well as MPs and ministers, don't really understand special schools and pupil referral units very well at all. After all, they've served their decade-and-a-half's worth of an apprenticeship of mainstream (or private school) observation, just like the rest of us. This helps explain comments such as 'How do we have ... run ... schools for children with special needs? How is that working?' by Nicky Morgan MP when she was asked about special schools by Laura McInerney, the editor of *Schools Week*, in an interview soon after the 2015 general election.[4] It could also be that they hold the view that a sector accounting for 1.1% of all children, most of whom do not currently go on to work or are, to use that most disparaging of phrases, economically inactive, is worth little in terms of time and thought.

There would be a risk in making special schools a central feature of a speech, as speakers' veneer of knowledge could rapidly disappear under any form of scrutiny. To be fair to her, Nicky Morgan did visit Swiss Cottage School, a special school, and Lord Nash visited The Bridge AP Academy, an alternative provision academy, both in London, soon after the 2015 general election.

Perhaps they believe that what happens in special schools has absolutely nothing to do with what happens in mainstream schools? After all, they account for 1.1% of the school-age population (but account for approximately 10% of all education spending). They may view it as an inefficient use of their time to focus on such a proportion of the population. Compare this possibility and weigh it up against the amount of time spent discussing how brilliant independent schools, which educate 7% of the school-age population, are, and how mainstream schools should be more like them as a counter-argument.

The Ofsted inspection framework is a mainstream construct into which other types of school have to fit. I can see how colleagues from other sectors or those looking in from outside the profession may think that the grade descriptors are overly easy on special schools and pupil referral units. Yet a glance at Ofsted's *School Inspection Handbook* shows the grade descriptors for the judgement on personal development, behaviour and welfare and it indicates how high the bar is set for the behaviour of students if a school is to be judged Outstanding:[5]

Outstanding (1)

- Pupils are confident, self-assured learners. Their excellent attitudes to learning have a strong, positive impact on their progress. They are proud of their achievements and of their school.

- Pupils discuss and debate issues in a considered way, showing respect for others' ideas and points of view.

- In secondary schools, high-quality, impartial careers guidance helps pupils to make informed choices about which courses suit their academic needs and aspirations. They are prepared for the next stage of their education, employment, self-employment or training.

- Pupils understand how their education equips them with the behaviours and attitudes necessary for success in their next stage of education, training or employment and for their adult life.

- Pupils value their education and rarely miss a day at school. No groups of pupils are disadvantaged by low attendance. The attendance of pupils who have previously had exceptionally high rates of absence is rising quickly towards the national average.

- Pupils' impeccable conduct reflects the school's effective strategies to promote high standards of behaviour. Pupils are self-disciplined. Incidences of low-level disruption are extremely rare.

- For individuals or groups with particular needs, there is sustained improvement in pupils' behaviour. Where standards of behaviour were already excellent, they have been maintained.

- Pupils work hard with the school to prevent all forms of bullying, including online bullying and prejudice-based bullying.

- Staff and pupils deal effectively with the very rare instances of bullying behaviour and/or use of derogatory or aggressive language.

- The school's open culture actively promotes all aspects of pupils' welfare. Pupils are safe and feel safe at all times. They understand how to keep themselves and others safe in different situations and settings. They trust leaders to take rapid and appropriate action to resolve any concerns they have.

- Pupils can explain accurately and confidently how to keep themselves healthy. They make informed choices about healthy eating, fitness and their emotional and mental well-being. They have an age-appropriate understanding of healthy relationships and are confident in staying safe from abuse and exploitation.

- Pupils have an excellent understanding of how to stay safe online and of the dangers of inappropriate use of mobile technology and social networking sites.

- Pupils' spiritual, moral, social and cultural development equips them to be thoughtful, caring and active citizens in school and in wider society.

This is a significant challenge for special schools, pupil referral units and, most obviously, schools that work either exclusively or with significant numbers of children who have social, emotional and mental health difficulties. Note that the descriptor does not allow for context. Use of words and terms such as 'pupils' impeccable conduct', 'incidences of low-level disruption are extremely rare' and 'pupils value their education and rarely miss a day at school' (average special school attendance in England is 91%) leave little room for nuance. At least the judgement does make some reference to children with particular needs.

Despite that challenge, the statistics are enlightening:

> 54% of all special schools have an Outstanding judgement for behaviour and safety.[6]

> 33% of all other schools have an Outstanding judgement for behaviour and safety.

> 27% of all pupil referral units have an Outstanding judgement for behaviour and safety.[7]

Outside the professional expertise contained within special schools, very few people have an appreciation of what good progress looks like, or how it can be assessed for children with complex learning difficulties and disabilities. Perhaps the common view is that anything that looks good is likely to be judged as such without a great deal of scrutiny? After all, would you *really* know what effective teaching looked like for someone with profound and multiple learning difficulties, or someone with extreme emotional and behavioural difficulties? If you watched a lesson in a sensory room, would you be impressed to see all sorts of lights, bubbles, sounds and vibrating chairs operating at the same time? The novice observer may well be impressed, and I've shown many visitors around the school where I was deputy head teacher who were also impressed, and it's easy to see why. I wouldn't. The most effective use of such resources I've seen has been when teachers use one specific piece of equipment – a head switch by which a child can turn a bubble tube on and off, for example – while all the other equipment is switched off. How is the child supposed to link their deliberate action of operating the head switch to the (de)activation of the bubble tube if there are four or five other sources of stimulation on the go at the same time?

Do inspectors really know what they're looking at when they inspect special schools? Laura McInerney, writing in the *Guardian* in January 2015,[8] provocatively, but correctly, questioned this:

> Instead of brilliant schools, could it be that inspectors are overly moved by a syrupy view of disability? When they observe happy children with

complex needs who appear to behave and look well treated, do inspectors whack out generous Outstanding judgements as a way of rewarding the school for relieving society of its guilt about what to do with disabled children, rather than basing the grading on whether students are being fully extended to learn?

You would expect the head teacher of a special school to put up a stout defence to support the view that they do, but that's precisely what my experience tells me.

We have just had the first year of another evolution of the inspection framework, but this one is different from many previous evolutions in that Ofsted are dispensing with the use of additional inspectors (AIs) subcontracted from inspection providers such as Tribal. Inspectors will now be one of two varieties – Her Majesty's Inspectors (HMI) or Ofsted inspectors (OIs). Ofsted helpfully publish pen portraits of their HMIs, but not OIs as of the time of writing, so I can't get a sense of how many of them have special school experience. Of the 172 HMIs, one describes herself (the portraits are mini-autobiographies) as having worked in a pupil referral unit, while ten have experience of working in special schools prior to joining Ofsted, three have worked as SENCos, and eight say they have experience of inspecting special schools. This is not an overwhelmingly large number, but it must be noted that HMI do not lead or carry out all inspections. My own experiences indicate that there is sufficient expertise out there, although I clearly can't guarantee that that has been the case in all inspections.

In the ten years that I have been a senior leader in special schools I have had:

- four full inspections (so-called section 5 inspections);
- two full residential care inspections (conducted annually for special schools that have residential facilities);
- one monitoring inspection (so-called section 8 inspections);
- section 5 inspection judgements ranging from Outstanding (one) to Good (two) to Requires Improvement (one).

The only time I have seen an HMI was for the section 8 monitoring inspection. All the other inspectors on all the other teams were of the now-defunct additional inspector (AI) variety. That amounts to nine

AIs. All, including the HMI, bar one, had considerable special school leadership experience and were impressive people. Only one AI gave me the impression that he wasn't completely confident about what he was looking at, despite considerable experience of inspecting special schools. We had a one-hour slot in which he was detailed to grill me about the progress our students were making. We had a long and wide-ranging discussion centred around the one thing we seemed to have in common – when he discovered that I live in Sandhurst, he waxed lyrical about the place, as he had lived there when his father had been posted to the Royal Military Academy as an army doctor many years ago. I suspected then – and still think now – that he had limited confidence in assessing the progress the students in the school were making.

I know that this generally positive experience is not shared by everyone. Matt Keer, parent of two children with SEN, recently submitted a Freedom of Information request to Ofsted in order to elicit details of the training that inspectors receive, following the inspection of his child's school.[9] Mr Keer was concerned that none of the inspectors had the qualifications, experience and expertise necessary to inspect the school properly, and sought to learn more about how inspectors are trained for this. Mr Keer asked 'How much time does Ofsted expect an HMI or AI to take to complete this enhanced [SEN] training programme, measured in days or hours?'

In response to Mr Keer's Freedom of Information request, Ofsted said:

> There are two parts to the enhanced training. All inspectors who inspect in specialist provision complete an initial day of enhanced training. This training was updated in light of amendments to the inspection handbook in September 2014, and the Code of Practice published by the Department for Education. It will be reviewed again this year in light of the Future of Education Inspection reforms currently being developed by Ofsted. In addition to this initial day specialist inspectors attend an additional training day each year, within which they focus on national developments in SEND and to specific areas of inspection. The focus of this day changes each year.

Almost all special schools will be without any cohort-scale external examination information that can be scrutinised (this is also true for nurseries, interestingly). How do we really know that the teachers in these schools are not being overly generous or protecting their own backs by inflating progress? This is a difficult one to challenge in terms of bald statistics, because there aren't any.

I have always said that the real test of the effectiveness of schools such as the one that I serve can be made when our students are 25. This does not sit well with the current political climate around schools, where the end point narrative, the headline results and the culture of performativity rule. No one will allow me to invite them back in nine years to see how our students really fared.

The framework accounts for this lack of external examination information. The inspectors I've dealt with, bar the one above, have demanded to know how assessments are moderated, by whom and how regularly. They have sought to check our assessment with the work the students are producing. They challenge us about our expectations of good or exceptional progress, which students we have identified who may be making slower than expected progress and, if so, how are we seeking to remedy that. (How to realistically define benchmarks such as 'expected progress' for children with learning difficulties of any severity is a topic that is crying out to be written about in a PhD thesis.) They also ask about the future of our students. In special schools, more than in any other sector, we understand how crucial it is for us to explicitly prepare our students to live and work independently, as this cannot be taken for granted.

The fact that special schools are so good at the promotion of independence, the development of work-related skills and the development of social communication skills is what makes their omission from one particular section of Ofsted's annual report for 2013/14 particularly irksome. There are three paragraphs in the section entitled 'Ensuring that pupils with special educational needs fulfil their potential' – and special schools are not mentioned once. The following paragraph from the 2013/14 annual report is by far the most irritating:[10]

> 42. Most schools monitor closely the progress that disabled pupils and those with special educational needs make in their academic subjects, especially in English and mathematics. However, less attention is paid to the progress they make in developing personal and social skills and in becoming more independent. Parents value these achievements highly and success in them can make a substantial difference to the young person's future. More attention should be paid to supporting pupils in these important aspects of their personal development.

It is irritating because special schools focus very successfully on precisely that to which Ofsted claims less attention is being paid. This may well be true in some mainstream schools – they are up against it in terms of their GCSE or SATs targets, so curriculum time is a precious commodity – and I think the first sentence should read 'Most mainstream schools monitor…' but special schools lead the way here. Special schools cannot function without a central focus on the development of independence in their students. Perhaps there is a risk there to Ofsted and the government. If they boldly assert that special schools have got it right and mainstream schools need to learn from them, then the retort will soon follow that this is incompatible with a congested mainstream curriculum, with the EBacc[11] and with Progress 8.[12] Schools would need to invest more time in an already crowded curriculum – which they cannot risk.

When I first joined our school in 2011 I asked all staff, parents, students and governors the same question: 'What should the students be able to do by the time they leave Carwarden House?' The parents were very clear on this: they expect us to do our utmost to enable their son or daughter to live and work independently.

The students' responses were remarkably similar. In the main, they wanted to be able to get a *paid* job, have a boyfriend or girlfriend, have their own flat and drive a car. Not too much to ask. The responses give us, and our school vision, a very clear direction, and a clear picture of what success looks like for our students. I have yet to visit a special school that does not operate along similar lines.

Many special school leaders know that some people – outside the special school community – think that inspection is an easier hurdle to negotiate if you're a special school. It is entirely predictable that I should seek to defend the record of the sector, so if Ofsted or the government believes in our success as much as we do, it is disappointing that they don't make more of it.

I last heard Ofsted blowing a trumpet to announce the success of special schools in 2009 when it published *Twelve Outstanding Special Schools: Excelling through inclusion*.[13] It is an exceptionally informative document which seeks to shine a light on the best out there. Dr Christine Gilbert was the Chief Inspector of Schools at the time, and part of her foreword is worth reproducing here.

> These schools are educational innovators. They have staff who are exceptionally skilled both as educators and as carers, and who have a passion for their work and a deep affection and respect for the children they teach. The teachers and support staff have a range of communication skills which enable them to connect with their students. Many teachers have a refined ability to recognise needs and responses which may be far from evident, enhanced teaching skills, and the expertise to recognise progress which may proceed in tiny increments. Some are required to have the experience, knowledge and versatility to provide, as part of a staff team, for all the main components of the 3 to 19 mainstream curriculum.
>
> One principle stands out. Those who work in these schools aim never to give up on a child. They have the highest aspirations for them and expect these children and young people to learn, achieve and succeed in different ways. In such a positive environment, the children and young people respond unusually well. This report illustrates many cases of young people who, from small beginnings or from schooling that was interrupted by obstacles and traumatic events, have gone on to achieve remarkable things. They demonstrate their school's success in improving their life chances, despite their circumstances.
>
> What these schools can do, others can. This document presents a challenge for special and hospital schools and pupil referral units which are not yet outstanding. Mainstream schools also have much to learn from some of the approaches described here.

When reading Ofsted's current publications, you could be forgiven for thinking that their remit does not extend to special schools. The fact that it does makes special schools' lack of prominence, despite their impressive outcomes in terms of inspection judgements, an issue that must be resolved to show the sector that it is still of value to the inspectorate.

I look forward to the day when Ofsted issues a direct challenge to mainstream schools to learn from those schools, and sees fit once more to shout from the rooftops about the successes of a sector that, by the judgements of its own inspectors, is doing remarkable things with some of society's most vulnerable and complex children.

What can be done to ensure special schools are inspected and supported in a fair, professional and meaningful way?

- Ofsted must now give parity to the specialist sector in its annual reports. The performance of special schools gets its own section in the 2014/15 report[14] that was released at the time of writing, and they make clear the reasons, leadership most notably, for the strong performance of the sector. It should prompt further discussion and debate about the reasons for the differences in outcome for different sectors. If it is true that the factors that make special schools successful when judged against the framework (and some of these reasons will also apply to nurseries) are not easily or cheaply reproducible in mainstream schools (I don't think they are), then the profession, its regulator and politicians should be grown-up enough to have this debate. A likely outcome of that debate would be a call in some quarters for separate frameworks for mainstream and specialist provision, as noted below.

- I believe the time has come for separate inspection frameworks so that the differences in performance measures between a tiny nursery and a 2,500-student secondary, for example, could be reflected in greater depth. This suggestion has implications for the workforce of inspectors who can currently inspect a very wide range of provision under the same document. A framework exclusively for specialist settings would likely contain a greater depth of measures of progress and would specifically reference the contribution of the therapists detailed above, for instance. This brings with it its own difficulties because inspectors of an educational provision would then be making judgements about the work of, in that case, health professionals – and this has clear training implications. The framework could, of course, expect the leaders of the schools to have this expertise and the inspectors would then merely need convincing of the accuracy of the schools' own internal judgements. A minimum level of knowledge would, though, be needed on the part of the inspectors in order to prevent an automatic rubber-stamping of a school's grading. Residential special schools already receive separate annual inspections of a different nature on the quality of their residential provision, as judged against the national minimum standards for boarding or residential special schools. These are still carried out by inspectors from Ofsted, but these professionals are social care regulatory inspectors who typically have social care backgrounds and qualifications.

- Ofsted's desire to see more serving leaders carrying out many more inspections is patently a good thing in terms of its ability to defend the credibility of its team in the field and their ability to make sound judgements. If there are sufficient serving leaders with the experience and knowledge of the special school sector in these teams then we can hopefully avoid any other parents having the same concerns that Matt Keer did (detailed on page 69).

Inspection and inclusion

Up until a few years ago, any use of the word 'outstanding' by an education professional would have passed without comment. Now it is a word so loaded with meaning that any utterance, especially by head teachers, is deliberate and dripping with intent. I have used it 62 times in this book, and writing it each time has left me feeling slightly unclean. Why unclean? Because to me it has become a form of professional vanity to describe an aspect of one's school as outstanding these days. I have come to detest the word and now regard it as the most toxic word in the vocabulary of schools today. Seeing the vision statement of one sentence of a school recently that contained the words 'outstanding school' and 'outstanding teaching' brought home to me that it is the only currency in town.

I made a commitment at the beginning of this academic year that I would not use either of the 'O' words – 'Ofsted' or 'outstanding' – at all at school, with the two exceptions of in senior leadership team and governing body meetings, but even in those situations I would never use it as an ambition. I must have used it excessively in the past, as a drinks coaster was made for me by a colleague with *OUTSTANDING* written across it in big letters – hearing you loud and clear, Houston.

I see two types of outstanding school, and have worked in one of each. There are the modest, low-key world beaters who are doing amazing things, day in, day out, but who haven't lost sight of their core purpose. The head teacher may take the Ofsted certificate that comes with the grade 1 judgement out of the drawer it's kept in occasionally and give it a little kiss, but it soon goes back into the darkness – and the exceptional business of the school carries on as usual.

For the other type, the school revolves around the word. Retention of that status has become the school's *raison d'être* and the Ofsted handbook that is written for inspectors has been eaten whole like a nauseating oyster and become the *How to Run an Outstanding School: the Haynes Owners' Workshop Manual for Head Teachers*. I recall the staff meeting we had on the eve of an inspection a few years ago. The head teacher's opening sentence to us all was '*I* [my emphasis added] can't be anything less than outstanding.'

My concern about the word has nothing to do with the desire of head teachers, senior leaders, governors, teachers, support staff and parents who want their schools to be of the highest possible calibre; it is that the blind rush to secure the coveted grade 1 badge of honour can have a disproportionately negative effect on the entitlement of children with learning difficulties.

Kristian Still, deputy head teacher of Wellington Academy in Wiltshire, and Phil Bourne, Director for School and Academy Compliance, have conducted a compelling analysis of the evidence which indicates a link between the prior attainment of children in a school and the school's grading by Ofsted. The work is detailed and the analysis very clearly laid out on Kristian's website,[15] so it won't be repeated here, but the conclusion is clear: 'Statistically, the scatterplots highlight that both Primary and Secondary schools with pupils with higher *prior* attainment profile, have a greater likelihood of getting better achievement outcomes and now as we observe their Ofsted Outstanding judgement. The converse is equally presented.'

The *TES* reported in November 2015 that a senior Ofsted official, Robert Pike, Ofsted's chief statistician, has said that it is 'harder' for schools with lower-ability intakes to gain Good or Outstanding judgements from the watchdog. Mr Pike also stated that it is 'probably easier' for 'schools with advantaged intakes' to receive Ofsted's top two grades.[16]

All head teachers understand that Ofsted inspections are now high-stakes set pieces. No matter how insignificant you try to make it for everyone else in your school, and I hope that you do, you cannot lose sight of the fact that your job is on the line if your school is judged badly. It is unfortunate but the grade of the school is inextricably linked to the person who is the head teacher at the time of the inspection. An inadequate school has an inadequate leader, so the logic goes. Speaking to a great group of parents of children with learning difficulties recently, I told them not to underestimate the power of the Ofsted inspection regime to influence and drive the behaviour of head teachers (think negative behaviour and unmet needs here, free-willers).

I used an example from my primary school days to illustrate the point. I used to play for our school football team when I was in primary school. Our head teacher coached us and he had one rule that was drilled in to us right from the start: 'If your knees aren't dirty at half-time you haven't been working hard enough,' he would boom at us. This thought used to creep up on me as the first half progressed, no doubt detracting from my focus on the game. I would check my knees repeatedly to avoid a public dressing-down at half-time. I distinctly remember once sliding for a ball that had long left the field of play in order to soil my knees just before half-time. It was regarded as a measure of success, so we did it. Winning 4-0? Losing 3-1? Didn't matter as long as those knees were filthy. The same applies to head teachers. If we know that someone is going to turn up periodically and look at our knees, then in order to keep our job or that coveted grade then we're going to damn well make sure that they are covered in mud.

If you are aware of the link between securing a strong judgement from Ofsted and the prior attainment of the children in your school then I can see how this can influence the willingness of head teachers to take on students with learning difficulties who are likely, by definition, to have relatively low prior attainment.

The Office of the Children's Commissioner produced a very balanced and impressive report in 2014 on the admissions practices of schools entitled 'It might be best if you looked elsewhere': an investigation into the *schools admission process.*[17] Further reference to it will be made in Chapter 5 on the effects on parents, but the following piece of evidence (which they gathered *from a practitioner*) is informative:

> I think it's the children with SEN, who would experience this type of discrimination most, right from the outset. If you've got a statement with quite significant needs, no one wants to touch you with a barge pole. Despite the fact that schools have the pupil premium, SEN budgets and the funding that comes with the statement, they just don't want the hassle, they just focus on the 5 A-C students, the ones that can bring the results and get them up the league tables.

How could changes to the Ofsted inspection framework improve inclusion?

- An inspection framework that unfairly advantages schools with a higher prior attainment profile must be changed. The playing field has a deadly slope and there is no change of ends at half-time to even things up. The reintroduction of a separate judgement for the outcomes of children with SEN would help here, but only if it had teeth. One used to exist, in among the 23 or so other judgements that the framework contained a few years ago, but it was just noise and was certainly not a limiting judgement – that is to say the grade for the overall inspection could not exceed the grade for that particular element of the inspection. Schools seem to sink on the basis of apparently poor results with children who are in receipt of free school meals, for example, because they are 'not closing the gap'. This group has become high-profile, and schools and inspectors need to pay similar attention to children with learning difficulties if the behaviour of head teachers is to change in any meaningful way. Any such decision would also have to take into account cases where schools have disproportionately low numbers of children with statements of special educational needs or EHCPs, or on SEN support, to find out *why* this is the case and disincentivise them from cherry-picking children to ensure a more favourable cohort.

- A knock-on from a zero sum accountability system in which schools can only improve at the expense of others increases the difficulty in the recruitment of head teachers. An adverse judgement from Ofsted usually results in the departure of the head teacher these days. The queue of candidates who are willing to lead a school in just such a position is highly likely to be a short one. The new head teacher needs the constitution of an ox if they are to hold their nerve and avoid adopting strategies that disadvantage children with learning difficulties (see Chapter 5 for a particular unsavoury example of this).

- I am one of many head teachers, some of whom lead schools with a grade 1 judgement, calling for the abolition of the Outstanding grade from Ofsted. I fully accept that the role of an inspectorate is to enforce a set of well-understood minimum standards, but to extend that to labelling degrees of performance above that is not only unnecessary, but damaging, for the reasons stated above. The grade ladder suggests to parents that there is a clear distinction between a school judged to be Good and one judged to be Outstanding. A superb now ex-governor at my school used to ask, 'So, Ofsted say we're a "good" school, right? In what areas are we "inadequate" and in what areas are we "outstanding"?' He understood that judgements about the performance of a complex organisation like a school cannot truly be distilled down into a single word. The reality is merely shades of grey.

- I would, in fact, go further than calling for the abolition of the Outstanding grade. I remain unconvinced that a complex organisation can be described by a single number and associated word (although it does make it easy to fit on a banner). Our school's most recent inspection judgement characterises us as a Good school. There are aspects of my school that *are* good, but there are other aspects that are exceptional, and others that are not good enough (and show me a school where this is not the case). I can go along with the grading of separate areas, imperfect as it undoubtedly is, but the artificial distillation of complexity and variability in performance does more harm than good. Schools could still be in a category of concern, as it were, if any of their judgements were below the minimum accepted standard, but only for that area, and it would prevent their areas of strength from being overshadowed by the overall judgement. I am alarmed that the Department of Health has seen fit to adopt exactly the same set of grade descriptors for its hospitals[18] and Her Majesty's Inspectorate of Constabulary (HMIC) does the same for police forces[19] (although HMIC grade three separate areas of performance), hospitals and police forces both being organisations that are several orders of magnitude more complex than schools. To try to describe these multidisciplinary public sector organisations in such a manner is like a daily public service announcement that proclaims, 'Today the air quality in England is good.'

Notes

1. Ofsted, *The Annual Report of Her Majesty's Chief Inspector of Education, Children's Services and Skills 2013/14* (2014). Available at: https://www.gov.uk/government/uploads/system/uploads/attachment_data/file/384699/Ofsted_Annual_Report_201314_HMCI_commentary.pdf.
2. See https://www.gov.uk/government/statistics/monthly-management-information-ofsteds-school-inspections-outcomes.
3. See https://www.gov.uk/government/publications/school-inspection-handbook-from-september-2015.
4. See http://schoolsweek.co.uk/schools-week-editor-interviews-edcuation-secretary-audio-recording/.
5. Ofsted, *School inspection handbook: Handbook for inspecting schools in England under section 5 of the Education Act 2005* (August 2015). Available at: https://www.gov.uk/government/publications/school-inspection-handbook-from-september-2015, p. 52.
6. 'Behaviour and safety' is used deliberately as opposed to 'personal development, behaviour and welfare', as it is now known in the Ofsted inspection framework, as that was its title when these schools were inspected.
7. See Management information – Schools – 30 September 2015 – https://www.gov.uk/government/statistics/monthly-management-information-ofsteds-school-inspections-outcomes.
8. L. McInerney, 'Top Ofsted rating for many SEN schools – so why aren't we trumpeting success?' *The Guardian* (20 January 2015). Available at: http://www.theguardian.com/education/2015/jan/20/ofsted-sen-schools-outstanding.
9. A. McGauran, 'Parents question inspectors' special needs training', *Schools Week* (17 April 2015). Available at: http://schoolsweek.co.uk/parents-question-inspectors-special-needs-training/.
10. Ofsted, *The Annual Report of Her Majesty's Chief Inspector of Education, Children's Services and Skills 2013/14* (2014). Available at: https://www.gov.uk/government/uploads/system/uploads/attachment_data/file/384699/Ofsted_Annual_Report_201314_HMCI_commentary.pdf, p. 16.
11. The English Baccalaureate (EBacc) is a performance measure for schools in England, first applied in the 2010 school performance tables. It measures the achievement of pupils who have gained Key Stage 4 (GCSE level) qualifications in the following subjects: English, mathematics, history or geography, the sciences, and a language.

12. A performance measure based on students' KS4 progress measured across eight subjects: English; mathematics; three other EBacc subjects (see above); and three further subjects, which can be from the range of EBacc subjects, or can be any other approved, high-value arts, academic or vocational qualification.
13. Ofsted, *Twelve Outstanding Special Schools: Excelling through inclusion* (2009), p. 2.
14. Ofsted, *The Annual Report of Her Majesty's Chief Inspector of Education, Children's Services and Skills 2014/15* (2015). Available at: https://www.gov.uk/government/uploads/system/uploads/attachment_data/file/483347/Ofsted_annual_report_education_and_skills.pdf, p. 60.
15. See http://www.kristianstill.co.uk/wordpress/2015/03/04/what-of-outstanding-schools-have-below-average-ability-intake/.
16. See https://www.tes.com/news/school-news/breaking-news/exclusive-brighter-pupils-make-getting-top-ratings-easier-ofsted.
17. Office of the Children's Commissioner, *'It might be best if you looked elsewhere'*, p. 24.
18. See http://www.cqc.org.uk/content/ratings.
19. See https://www.justiceinspectorates.gov.uk/hmic/peel-assessments/peel-2015/.

Chapter 5

Roadkill Littering the Highway to Outstanding

'We must love one another or die.'

W.H. Auden, 'September 1, 1939'

I have the pleasure of visiting the world-class Moorfields Eye Hospital in London twice a year so that my daughter can undergo the regular series of tests and check-ups that her congenital condition demands. We make a day of it, partly to take advantage of being in London, but principally to assuage the guilt that comes with taking your child for a series of medical tests, some invasive, on a regular basis.

Soon after my daughter's birth my wife and I noticed that one of her pupils was milky and opaque; a fact that was unfortunately missed during her post-birth midwife check. A visit to the GP confirmed what we suspected – or so we thought: the presence of a congenital cataract. A visit to a paediatrician a few weeks later backed this up. 'Yup, that's a cataract. We'll get the expert doctors at Moorfields to whip that out, put an artificial lens in and we're done.'

A visit to Great Ormond Street for my daughter to have sensors placed all over her tiny head and a stroboscope flashed in her face for an electroencephalogram ('She's sleeping. Would you like me to wake her?' 'No. The light goes through the eyelids. Keep feeding her that bottle, it's keeping her still.') indicated that there was more to this milky pupil than there first appeared. Our appointment coincided with the presence of a gaggle of TV crews at the entrance to the hospital because of the death of one of a pair of conjoined twins at the hospital that day. As a reminder of the need to keep things in perspective, it couldn't have been more stark.

Our first visit to Moorfields afterwards confirmed the absence of a cataract as the consultant said, virtually from the other side of the room:

'Ah, I see that one of your daughter's eyes is smaller than the other.'

'Er, really?'

'Yes. It's obvious.'

It wasn't.

'I spend all day looking at eyes. Take a really good look and you'll see.'

It was.

An ultrasound revealed the problem. I learned that the condition meant that my daughter was blind in one eye and that eye was microphthalmic – that is, smaller than normal. It meant that she would have to wear a prosthesis in that eye to bring it up to full size. Failure to do this would affect that part of her skull, as we found that the eyeball grows and forces that part of the skeleton to grow. The milky appearance was caused by the presence of the calcified hyaloid artery, which normally dissolves before birth. Hers remained, but could be removed by surgery, but she would still be blind in that eye. The cause was likely to be chickenpox (which my son caught while my wife, who had already had chickenpox, was pregnant with my daughter).

I'm a good listener but the consultant, Mr Moore, must have thought me very rude as I constantly interrupted him with questions. The first one, 'Does this condition have any learning difficulties associated with it?' left my mouth almost before he had started talking. As it was becoming clear that this wasn't a simple 'milky lens out, bionic lens in' routine, I started to wonder if my daughter had a condition that would affect her cognitive development. I wish to make it clear that I wasn't worried about having a child with learning difficulties. My feelings were much more selfish than that. I didn't want to have to be one of the formidable band of people who are the parents of children with intellectual or physical disabilities, who have to expend a disproportionate amount of energy, emotion and, in some cases, money to fight for their child's basic entitlements. I have worked with – and got to know very well – many such parents over the years, and they are an inspiring group of people, but I have seen the toll that it can take and I had no desire to get any closer to it. I knew full well that there is a world of difference between working with children with learning difficulties and being the parent of a child with learning difficulties. One comes with a salary, a pension and several weeks off a year. The other does not.

We were lucky that day. Mr Moore was exceptional: sensitive, a clear communicator and a good listener. He advised us brilliantly: 'It's your choice. In five minutes you'll meet with the surgeon. He is going to persuade you to operate. Surgeons love to operate, but the decision is yours. You've heard all the facts, so make your own mind up and stick to it.'

I have never had a more important conversation with a professional about either of my children before or since. Why on earth would my wife and I have the temerity to go against the advice of an ophthalmic surgeon? Without that conversation, in which we were given very clear encouragement (it felt like permission, at the time) to form our own view and stick to it, we would have respectfully agreed with the surgeon and consented to whatever he recommended. Mr Moore remains the model to which I aspire when I meet parents at my school. We carefully considered the options and made up our minds. The surgeon didn't operate.

At our last visit to Moorfields, I sat next to two parents with babies who were at the beginning of the journey we've been on as a family for the past few years. One of the babies had one eye, and one baby had no eyes at all. A number of other children present had obvious learning difficulties. The lives of these parents will undoubtedly be punctuated by meetings and appointments with health and/or social care and/or education professionals in which they will have to tell their story time after time after time. All parents have hopes and dreams for their children, and these parents will constantly reassess their dreams for their children as they wonder whether their child will be able to live independently, go to university, get a job, get married, have their own children. It is what one parent once described to me as an 'extended grief', and a failure to understand it as such is likely to result in the needs of the whole family going unrecognised and unmet. Think about those unmet needs the next time you find yourself with a parent who you think is behaving unreasonably when discussing the needs of their child.

I first tuned in to this as a deputy head teacher when I used to show parents around our school on two or three occasions a week. Tears were common, as parents explained the battles they had fought, the bureaucracy they'd had to negotiate, and the money they'd had to spend on solicitors and barristers for tribunals. These tours were the first time that I really spent any decent time with parents that wasn't fully 'staged'. In secondary schools I rarely saw parents, certainly didn't call them, and then filled parents' evening appointments with inane teacher speak.

The parents of a child with any sort of disability need space. They need someone to listen, and you have to listen very carefully, otherwise there is a danger that you will begin to tune out, to start thinking of your next meeting or of that email that you really must send. You could quite easily fall into a 'parent tour fatigue' or a state of near hibernation where you go on to autopilot and forget how crucial these meetings are to parents. You would become the priest in Ireland – the most Catholic of countries – who conducted my grandfather's funeral and used a plastic dishmop instead of an aspergillum to spread holy water on my grandfather's coffin. I considered this act so disrespectful that it left me lost for words. The priest was suffering from funeral fatigue and treated it as just another job, forgetting its significance to everyone else in the building. The effects were lasting: the next time I was in that church, 14 years later for my grandmother's funeral, the first thing I did was to look for the aspergillum. Thankfully it was there – but the same priest wasn't. It was a different one this time (a lovely one, thankfully).

You need to actively seek to understand the parents and their situation. They can feel crushed by the weight of the system and exhausted by their journey as a lone voice, a fatigued but valiant advocate for their child. I was taught a lesson once by a parent for failing to listen attentively enough to him, or to read his body language. Fortunately for me, he was bold enough to tell me that to my face. He was explaining to me that his teenage son was just starting to have 'toddler tantrums' (his words). I made some sympathetic noises, for I was a parent too by now, but he cut me dead.

'You're not listening to me, are you? You think I'm moaning; I'm not. I'm delighted this is happening. I've waited 14 long years to see my son reach this step. It's progress. It means that he is learning that he can exert some control over what happens to him, and this is his way of telling me.'

That put me very firmly in my place.

Sometimes schools, perhaps with the best intentions, become insensitive to the needs of parents, and relationships can be damaged. I was shocked by a particularly poor example of home–school communication recently. I was part of a panel that was reviewing applications from schools for students to be granted statements of SEN, just before the advent of EHCPs. The school of the student in question used a system to text parents. Many schools use these as standard for generic messages and reminders, and they can be very efficient. For this child the school used it to enable adults in the class to text the parent – initially, I suppose, to communicate how the day had gone. The weighty pile of papers for this child contained a detailed log of all the texts the school had sent the mother – effective communication, you might say. The log started in a very positive way, but gradually took on a more blunt tone over time. One text stood out, and I reproduce it below exactly as it was written:

Your child is currently running around outside with no clothes on.

Present tense. No name. Perhaps the parent had more than one child in the school? No thought had been given to that. The use of the word *'your'* here seems loaded too. There was no mention of their mood either. Traumatised? Laughing? No thought had been given to how the parent would receive this message. My first thought on reading it was to wonder why a member of staff was busy typing out a text message to the parent instead of dealing with the child. This thought was immediately followed by disappointment that the school chose to text this kind of news to the parents instead of making a phone call. Insensitivity and thoughtlessness can cause irreparable damage to the relationship a school has with parents.

If you feel that you have parents that you would regard as 'pushy' – for that is the adjective of choice – then take a moment to appreciate their situation if you consider them unreasonable. They genuinely want to build a trusting partnership – they are not actively seeking conflict. They want the best for their child. They are likely to always have one eye on the future and know how critical it is to get the right provision for the child to maximise their chances of living and working independently (see Chapter 4 for how we asked for input from parents when forming our school vision). They have recognised how futile it is for them to join in with other parents and compare the development of their children. Requests for their child's speech and language therapy, occupational therapy or physiotherapy entitlement to be met – all common sources of frustration – are rooted in the knowledge that these will improve their child's ability to communicate, and to improve their fine motor skills, balance, fitness and dexterity. Parents know how critical these things are to achieving future independence; to retaining their child's dignity because they don't require assistance with their intimate care needs; to improving their chances of securing paid employment.

I talked to a number of parents in preparation for this book to elicit their experiences (both positive and negative) of choosing schools for their children with special needs, and what they had to say below shows how the staff working in schools can (either deliberately or inadvertently) reject children and their families, causing lasting damage.

A parent, a deputy head teacher no less, of a child with Down syndrome expressed concern to me that their child would occupy too much of the teacher's time and that the other children would suffer as a result. I did my best to reassure them and to tell them that a teacher would learn a lot about themselves and should become a better teacher for teaching someone with Down syndrome. I also explained that there would be no negative impact on the children. They would view the child's presence as a positive thing, as they would with any other child, and would embrace their place in the class.

I was struck by this parent's concern for the other children, seemingly before the parent's own, and I've not experienced this overtly before or since.

A parent of a child with learning and physical difficulties explained to me that:

> the junior school my child attended never wanted to understand my child's needs. I felt that, if they listened, it involved more work which they didn't want to do. They were rarely available to discuss, and if they were nothing was ever done. ... I was told that my child wouldn't be able to do swimming lessons, but could only go if I could be their one-to-one and take time off work. When my child was in Year 6 I was told that they wouldn't be in the Year 6 leavers' assembly play. I was devastated as my child loves being on stage and in plays. How could they expect my child to sit and watch their peers perform and they watch and wonder why they're not in it? I said they had to be in the play, and I wasn't happy. They had to adhere to what I said and my child was then in the play. My child remembered their lines and loved it. They were great,

and it made the school eat their words! I was also told they couldn't go on the residential trip. My child also wasn't allowed to join in with PE activities, so therefore socially wasn't encouraged. My child always did activities with a one-to-one teacher; they didn't give my child a chance. My child was always either in a corridor with a TA or even on their own, so socially they were very left out.

It gets worse:

Three weeks after my child had started in junior school I was asked to come in by the head teacher. It was such an unexpected upset: the head teacher told me in a heartless manner that it wasn't the right school for my child, and that I needed to look for another school. Her people skills and manner were disgraceful – it was such a shock, as they didn't even know my child at that point. I said no [HURRAH!], that for the time being my child was happy and did have friends, and was happy to come to school, and there wasn't another suitable school for them for now. The following day there was a list of special schools in my child's bag for me to go and have a look at! This continued until the Year 5 review where I involved the Parent Partnership Service and the local education authority, where it was agreed by them, not the head teacher, for my child to stay where they were as I had already made up my mind that they were to go to a secondary special school. Should a suitable special school have been available from Year 5, I would have transferred my child there and then.

When parents have to defend their child against such exclusive practices, it is no wonder they feel they have to bang the table just that little bit more firmly. To then label them as 'pushy' is rather sticking the knife in.

However, there are schools out there doing great things, and some parents reported to me some very positive experiences:

When they were in mainstream classes with support, my child was deliberately placed in classes with the most aware and experienced class teachers. We had occasional trouble with supply teachers or teachers who covered for the class teacher in their planning, preparation and assessment (PPA) time, but otherwise the staff's awareness of need and communication with parents and specialists was excellent across the school. The specialist unit staff were also proactive in investigating unmet needs – they encouraged us to seek an occupational therapy (OT) referral for our child's concentration problems, for example, and once we had the OT referral and a sensory diet in place, their concentration improved rapidly. The staff were very collaborative and interested in our experiences at home, and actively encouraged visits from other professionals involved in our child's disabilities.

We can be confident that there are many schools out there (I've visited some of them) who operate in this way. The law of unintended consequences takes over at this point, though. The school described above will get a well-deserved reputation locally as a school where the needs of young people with learning difficulties are well understood and where they make good progress. This can be exploited by other schools, perhaps ones that like to describe themselves as 'academic', who may persuade parents that 'it might be best if they looked elsewhere', as the title of the Office of the Children's Commissioner's report (see Chapter 4) tells us. Some of the evidence contained in this report is quite damning.[1]

> One practitioner told researchers:
>
> I think it's quite reasonable for schools to say, 'We don't have many Traveler children, or autistic children, or EAL children at the school and we know of other schools in the local area which do, have you considered applying to those?' As a parent I'd want to know that, I wouldn't see it as discriminatory, but some families, who face prejudice on a regular basis, might perceive it like that.

In the report another parent recalls:[2]

> When I went for the first visit to go and have a look at [the school], the lady made it clear as day that [my son] just wasn't going there. It was very unfair for them just to look at him in that one instance; he'd never been in that situation before. She took one look at us and she made that decision, 'No, he's not coming to this school, he wouldn't be able to cope, he would struggle. It might be best if he didn't come here. He'd be better off at a special needs school rather than here.' She made that decision without involving anyone else – just made that decision by looking at us. This really upset me. I thought if they are going to do that by just giving you a look, then is it worth him going to that school? I don't want to put him somewhere where he isn't going to be happy.

Mission accomplished for the school.

The same parent who reported to me the positive experience above of their child being placed in classes with the most aware and experienced class teachers still had some concerns:

> In retrospect, there was indirect resistance born out of honest motivations. For example, there was a definite culture at annual review meetings of talking up my child's achievements, concentrating on successes, and downplaying problematic areas. This wasn't meant to frustrate or deny my child's needs – it was simply about maintaining a positive

attitude – but I think that it made it harder to address poorly met areas of need quickly and forcefully.

This parent raises the point that other parents can have an impact on the acceptance – or not, as we shall see – of their child into the school community. The school can be doing all it can, can be a very inclusive educational establishment, and yet may be completely unable to control the actions and views of a significant proportion of its community. Crucially, too, the school can do nothing about the transmission of those prejudices and views outside the school day. I asked parents, 'Have you ever met any resistance from other parents regarding your child playing with their child, invitations to birthday parties or sleepovers, etc.?'

Here are the answers I received from the parent of two deaf children.

> Yes. Active, sustained resistance from other parents. Not because of my children's behaviour (which stayed the right side of fair-to-good throughout their time in mainstream), but because of their disability.
>
> Throughout their time in mainstream, my eldest got one invitation to a birthday party (whole class, age five). My youngest never got an invite. No after-school play, no sleepovers.
>
> Each year, we held a birthday party for each kid in the sports centre in the school's catchment (five miles away from our house). Each year, we invited the whole class. Each year – without fail – only one child would come: the other deaf child in their class. We had family friends at the parties – so there wasn't a complete no-show – but this got much harder as the children became more socially aware.
>
> The tipping point for us was when my youngest asked their classmates why they didn't come. They told him that their mum or dad had said no. One child tearfully told our youngest that she really wanted to come, but her dad had said that she wasn't going to go to a party with 'a child like that'. There is no way of explaining that to a child with a disability that doesn't make you despair for humanity.
>
> The school was in a multicultural, multi-social-class area. The kids were, almost without exception, lovely – but they came from cultures and social groups where revulsion over disability was strong. Parents would usher their kids away when our kids tried to communicate with them at school pick-up. This wasn't by any means a crude clash of cultural perceptions – some of the people most obviously revolted by my kids' disabilities were self-styled upstanding white middle-class Christian shoppers – but the impact on my kids was largely the same either way.
>
> For a while, my eldest was in a class with a kid who had recently arrived from a Middle Eastern country. The kids got on well – this child had a

natural gift for communicating with deaf children. Whenever I picked my kids up from school, my eldest would wave at this kid's mum, and she'd respond by tapping her head when walking away. I thought she was trying to sign to my eldest. I asked a colleague at work who came from the same region whether he knew anything about this sign. It turned out that what she was doing was warding off the 'evil eye' – the evil eye, of course, being my child. Again, there is no way of explaining that to a child with a disability that doesn't make you despair for humanity.

The school did its level best to make itself an inclusive, prejudice-free environment. But it was only one source of influence on the kids, and as they became older, many of the kids themselves started to distance themselves from mine, and take on the prejudices they were exposed to at home.

Since being at special school, the boys have not had any problems like this. Not once.

I also asked this parent if they felt that their school's head teacher worried that the school's Ofsted rating could be put at risk by having children with SEN on roll. (Note that this parent was also a governor at the school.)

Yes. The school never said this explicitly, but if you look at its actions at crucial points in my kids' education, you can see the impact – and it was nearly devastating. Here's why.

My child's school was placed into a category of concern by Ofsted (not Special Measures, but Notice to Improve). The report identified the deaf unit as an area requiring particular improvement. The unit wasn't inspected by anyone from Ofsted who knew anything about the disability, how to deliver provision well, or how kids like mine typically progress over time with the right support. But the data looked bad.

So the head was defenestrated. I had joined as a governor a few weeks before the inspection. I was one of the few who didn't resign, but the governing body was obviously very different thereafter. Working with the local authority, we brought in an interim leadership team whilst we set about recruiting a new head teacher for the next academic year.

This interim team knew just what it took to get the school out of that category. The team included someone who had done time as an additional Ofsted inspector, and their course was clear; the school's data had to show that rapid, sustained progress was happening.

Now unfortunately, at this time my eldest was in crisis. His cochlear implant had just failed – this implant is a key part of the equipment he needs to manage his disability, get access to sound, and acquire language. He needed a major operation to replace it. After the operation, he would not be able to make proper use of the implant straight away – he had to undergo a lengthy programme of intensive, specialised rehabilitation, much like how an amputee learns how to use a prosthetic limb.

So we drew up the programme: the hospital, his therapists, his teachers, and his parents, all working together from deep knowledge of his needs and the nature of the disability. This programme – slow, grinding, but effective – was the only way he would be able to restore his ability to access language over the long-term. If the programme was carefully managed, then he would only have six months where he didn't have usable hearing. If we didn't manage it carefully, there was a risk that he'd never get usable hearing back in the same way.

But there was a big problem. The programme would not give the specialist teacher and the deaf unit the opportunity to demonstrate that my eldest was making 'rapid, sustained progress'. And that was a big problem for the school and its interim leaders. They knew what Ofsted expected – and what they expected to see was 'rapid, sustained progress'.

So the school gave my eldest's specialist teacher a choice: junk the rehabilitation programme, or face capability. Make those two sub-levels of progress on paper, or never darken their door again. In terms of hearing, my eldest had just experienced the equivalent of an amputation, and was learning how to walk again. But what the school needed was different – they needed him to tap-dance at a demented tempo, simply so that their pivot table didn't have any awkward anomalies in it.

So the specialist teacher junked the programme. At an enormous cost to our eldest's long-term progress. He got his two sub-levels of progress on paper, but only by distorting his literacy development beyond reasonable shape. I would estimate that it took him twice as long to recover usable hearing and receptive language skills as it would otherwise have done.

I complained to the governing body – discreetly, but without effect. The need to get the school out of its Ofsted category trumped everything else. A few months later, we got the school out of category, and a new head teacher was appointed. A few weeks later, once the dust had settled, I resigned as a governor.

This isn't quite the question you asked – but it is a painful example of how perceived and actual pressure from Ofsted warps the judgement of school leaders, and damages the outcomes of children with special needs. It has also left me with a lifelong suspicion of anyone and anything involved in school improvement. At one of the most vulnerable and crucial moments in my son's life, he was treated like garbage for a meaningless greater good – like roadkill littering the highway to Outstanding.

One of the outcomes of school leaders behaving in the ways described above is the collateral damage it can have. Inexperienced teachers may well develop the view that this is how things are done. One parent recalls in the Office of the Children's Commissioner's report:

> I heard a newly qualified teacher say 'the parents chose this school; he has to fit in.' I think that was the first time they got a full lecture on children's rights and how we need to adapt our learning and reflect on our practice to enable them to have the right to an education at the level they need.

I was fortunate to listen to a very engaging and persuasive talk by Nick Hodge, Professor of Inclusive Practice at Sheffield Hallam University's Institute of Education, and Dr Katherine Runswick-Cole, Senior Research Fellow from Manchester Metropolitan University's Department of Psychology, on conversations between parents and professionals. They talked of the tensions that can sometimes arise, the reluctance of either party to say what they really think, and the danger of reading too much into another's words.

Some of the examples were overt. When a head teacher suggests that the school down the road 'does autism/challenging behaviour/Down syndrome better than we do' the message is not a subtle one (see also Chapter 4, pages 76–77). When a parent offers up a book on Prader–Willi syndrome to the class teacher, as has happened to me, and suggests they read it, the teacher may consider that an attack on their professional knowledge. The parent may well be genuinely attempting to help the teacher further their understanding. After all, how many mainstream colleagues have worked with a child with a rare syndrome before? Few. It could be, too, that the parent is saying in a roundabout way that the teacher hasn't been listening to the parent's advice for the past two years. The book is the last resort – 'Read that if you won't listen to me.'

If you end up teaching my daughter, this is likely to happen to you. You will be given an explanation about persistent hyperplastic primary vitreous (PHPV), how it affects my daughter, and the minor modifications you'd need to make to where she needs to sit in the class in relation to the board and to where adults would need to stand when talking to her, to ensure she wasn't significantly disadvantaged. I have no expectation that any teacher would know about PHPV, so I would approach this in the spirit of helping both my daughter and the teacher, but I can see how the teacher may well become defensive or dislike feeling that they are being told how to do their job.

It can feel like a win–lose situation. If you want to win then they have to lose, and most of us don't like losing. Those of us who work with students with extreme behavioural needs try to avoid zero sum situations (where for the teacher to win the student must seemingly lose) as some students will go to great lengths to avoid losing, failure or loss of face. Professor Hodge and Dr Runswick-Cole reminded me once again that we need to acknowledge the experiences, struggles and battles that many parents have been through to get to that point.

This can lead, in some cases, to parents being unaware where their child's school is located. This sounds impossible, but I have known two sets of parents at my current school who do not know where their child's school is. This is astounding, but there are perfectly logical explanations for this. It can be difficult for some parents to accept that their child goes to a special school. In these cases, I find that they haven't visited prior to admission, and don't attend parents' evening, annual reviews or any other opportunities to visit. They have simply accepted the local authority's offer of a place for their child at our school, or accepted by default by not replying to the letter. It is also possible that they were completely uninvolved in the selection of the school for their child. My contention is that they are attempting to retain an image in their mind of where their child goes to school, and I suspect that that image looks like a mainstream secondary school. Far better, surely, to maintain that image than shatter the illusion by seeing the school for real, goes the logic. The fact that transport is normally provided from a pupil's front door to the school gate and the distance to school can be large (my students travel to school every day from an area that covers a staggering 1,200 square miles, compared to six square miles for our local secondary school) makes this gulf harder to bridge.

When I first became a head teacher my first cohort of Year 7 pupils were bringing with them, so I was led to believe, two sets of parents who had reputations for advocating a little too strongly, shall we say, for their children. I have a policy of calling all the parents of new children in the school at the end of every September to gauge how they and their child are settling in to their new community. I was wary of calling these parents – looking back now, I don't know why I was so reticent – and left one of them to the very last. Soon after the conversation started the parent was in tears. Years of frustration, worry and stress were in there, that much was obvious.

I met both sets of parents personally soon after both children started. Both sets of parents had clearly been through very difficult times to battle for their children's basic entitlement to attend a suitable primary school. They simply wanted what was best for their children, and had to resort to advocating more strongly than should be necessary. In their shoes, I would have done exactly the same thing.

Far from taking an adversarial approach to the school, I found them warm and engaging, knowledgeable and altruistic. This is my kind of parent. I can use this kind of emotional energy, and these two parents are now vice-chairs of our governing body – and two of our best advocates. One said recently that she felt our school was unique. I asked her to expand on this with the staff, and she explained that we are open-minded, honest with parents and very welcoming. This obviously pleases us greatly, but while there are parents out there who don't even know where their child's school is, we have much more to do.

What can we do to make parents of children with learning difficulties feel more welcome in schools?

- We can all read 'What am I?' in the introduction again, and remember that the stress and worry that those statistics must cause for parents of children with learning difficulties is ever-present. My children are still young, but I have long since taken it for granted that they will have the ability and independence to live and work independently one day. I don't need to worry about how they will cope after I die, but I can assure you that that is something these parents ask themselves frequently. These parents need us. They need us to be on their side. Importantly, they need to feel that we are on their side. There will inevitably be tensions or differences of opinion at times, but I have found parents very willing to work with us when we admit that, even as a special school, we don't know everything and could learn a lot from them. They are, after all, experts on their own children. As the saying goes, 'If you've met one child with autism, then you've met one child with autism.' That means, each child with autism is different and has different needs. There is no manual that tells you how to teach all children with a particular condition. This sounds obvious, but if you tell a teacher that they will have a child in their class next year with Prader–Willi syndrome, for example, their initial reaction may be to say that they've never taught a child with such a condition before and don't know where to begin (see Chapter 1 for when I did precisely that). Of course, there are general things that teachers must know about any particular condition, but it does not follow that all children with a particular condition will be the same and should be taught in the same way. Far from it! I have worked with a small number of children over the years who have Down syndrome, and who also have ADHD and autism: three very different conditions, all wrapped up in one child who, before we even consider the distinct needs of those conditions, has their own unique personality, interests, strengths and foibles.

- The best schools have transition down to a fine art. They invest significant time and effort in ensuring children and staff have a good appreciation of each other before their relationship formally begins in September. I have come to realise over the years that I did not pay enough (or any, if I'm honest) attention to the transition process for parents. The parents of children with learning difficulties have been thinking and worrying about transitions (either starting school for the first time, or moving between schools or from school to college) long before their children knew what a secondary school or further education college is. Once a placement is agreed in our school (usually in the January of Year 6 or Year 11), we operate an open-door policy for parents. Some don't feel the need to visit again, whereas others visit a few times. They ask if they can bring siblings or grandparents for a tour and we encourage this – it allows them all to have conversations with the child about the school at regular intervals before September arrives. We also encourage them to take pictures to use as a focus for discussion at home. Having been to us and met us all, they can take a full part in the conversation, rather than just being told about the swimming pool or the pond, for example. They can also reassure the child about any concerns they may have. It is common for staff from the child's primary school to visit too, and to produce transition or moving-on booklets full of pictures and key information. This is crucial to reducing the anxiety of the child (and the parent, in almost all cases) about starting in a new place. Think of the last time you started a new job. Was it stress-free? I don't think so. If we can answer as many of the parents' and children's questions as possible – Where are the toilets? What does the head teacher look like? Where is my form room? Who is my form tutor? Where is my locker? Where do I eat lunch? – then Year 7 starts as smoothly as possible.

- We must ensure that we don't, inadvertently or otherwise, exclude children from certain activities (as noted by the Contact a Family survey back in Chapter 3). There can be no justification for leaving a child out of the Year 6 leavers' assembly (as noted above), or for setting parental attendance as a precondition for going on a residential trip. If extra support is required, then local authorities have mechanisms by which funding can be, and is, provided, even for short-term needs such as a residential trip.

- We can harness parents' energy, determination and knowledge to our advantage – for they have all three in abundance. It took me many years as a teacher to really know anything about school governance, and for a while I thought it overrated.[3] Now I would feel quite exposed without a strong governing body. One of our school's strengths is the contribution our parents make, some of whom are mentioned above. I know they also feel a deep sense of satisfaction from being able to support and influence a system they felt wasn't listening to them for years.

Notes

1. Office of the Children's Commissioner, *'It might be best if you looked elsewhere': an investigation into the schools admission process* (2014). Available at: https://www.childrenscommissioner.gov.uk/sites/default/files/publications/It_might_be_best_if_you_looked_elsewhere.pdf, p. 25.
2. Office of the Children's Commissioner, *'It might be best if you looked elsewhere'*, p. 27.
3. See https://www.tes.com/news/school-news/breaking-views/five-ways-heads-turn-governors-a-critical-friend.

Chapter 6

Herd Immunity

'Another conference, another tour. Here the buzz theme was "the Disabled". But why? It's the *able* I want to get back into work. If civil servants think their career prospects are centred around what they can do
for the disabled, that is what they will focus on. But it all causes long-
term dilution. Society will become an inverted pyramid with the whole
load of pensions, benefits and hand-outs for minorities being carried by
a few tough and house-proud workers. This is the kind of thing I went
into politics to stop.'[1]

Rt Hon. Alan Clark MP, Minister for Employment, 1983

In the past few years, there has been a rise in the number of cases of
measles in the United Kingdom. The reduction in the percentage of children being vaccinated, either with the triple vaccine for measles, mumps
and rubella (MMR) or with the single measles vaccine, makes it easier
for the virus to spread, and this has prompted action from policy-makers
and health professionals. People are still wary of the MMR, thanks to
the research of now discredited gastroenterologist Andrew Wakefield
in 1998, in which he stated that autism could be caused by the MMR
vaccine.

Vaccination works on herd immunity, meaning that a certain percentage
of the population needs to be vaccinated to make it extremely difficult
for the virus to spread. This varies from virus to virus, but for measles
herd immunity is achieved when 95% of the population are vaccinated.
Following the publication of Wakefield's study, vaccination levels for
MMR dropped significantly, falling to a rate of 80% in 2003. Given the
difference between the desired 95% and the reality, you can see why this
caused a public health problem. Seventeen years later, we still have issues
with persuading people to give their children the triple vaccine – as the
fear lives on.

In the case of measles, 95% can be effectively considered to be *all* a population: 5% of the population can be unvaccinated, but they are protected by those who are vaccinated.

In the field of education, it is obvious that the only figure we should regard as acceptable when formulating policy for children is 100%. It seems evident that no education policy should deliberately exclude or disadvantage a certain portion of the population – but this does happen.

Unfortunately politicians do create policies that exclude a certain percentage of children and leave them exposed to the symptoms of the metaphorical policy virus. In some cases, politicians are perfectly aware that a policy disadvantages a percentage of the population, such as the Year 1 Phonics Check or the changes to terminal examinations and removal of coursework for GCSE. In other cases the realisation is retrospective, but it is too late and generally no remedial action follows.

I contend that children with learning difficulties and disabilities and SEN are most negatively affected by such political decisions. It is an inevitable consequence of a system that seeks to portray itself as academic, that regards the word 'vocational' as a proxy for second-class qualifications that are considered easy or lacking in rigour, and that regards anything below 32 (currently) in the Year 1 phonics screening check, what used to pass for Level 4 in Year 6 or grade C at GCSE as failure.

In *The Sunday Times* on 1 February 2015, the then Secretary of State for Education Nicky Morgan was quoted as saying that she would:

> launch a war on illiteracy and innumeracy ... We will expect every pupil by the age of 11 to know their times tables off by heart, to perform long division and complex multiplication and to be able to read a novel. They should be able to write a short story with accurate punctuation, spelling and grammar.[2]

It is concerning that a minister deliberately used the words 'launch a war'. Britain declares war, extremely rarely, on other countries or terrorists, yet the Secretary of State for Education used such language in an article in which the teaching profession took a hammering. These children aren't doing well enough because we're not good enough.

I used to believe, naïvely, that Mrs Morgan, despite her position, was probably completely unaware that there are children in this country who are 11 years old but who, for many reasons (none of which are the fault of their teachers and parents), cannot do those things she mentioned at the standard she demands. They may have profound and multiple learning difficulties, and have reached a level of development that would be considered typical for a 12-month-old, say, and there are thousands of other reasons why. I no longer believe that she was unaware of this. So why make a speech deliberately using the language of *all* when she probably has no expectation that all children can, or will, achieve such a goal?

We are partly complicit. We have played a part in bringing this situation about because of the relationship we have as a nation with politicians. We don't like it when they change their minds. Smart leaders in all professions do it when they can see they've made a mistake or circumstances have changed. When new evidence comes along, we should reassess to make sure we're on the right track. Yet we charge politicians with weakness when they change their mind. This encourages entrenchment and an unwillingness to change tack, even when it is the right thing to do. We also prefer them to sound as if they have firm convictions, that they are uncompromising on standards, and that they expect the best. This is where the language of *all* creeps in. Speeches and articles that contain phrases such as 'most children will …' sound half-hearted and lacking in aspiration. Opposition spokespersons pounce on such language with: 'They say *most*. Well, we say *all*'. Consequently, politicians use the language of *all*.

But why is this important?

The language of *all* in this case excludes a proportion of children, by definition. No one who knows anything about children will believe that any education system can teach every single 11-year-old in the land to learn their multiplication tables up to 12 off by heart, or to perform long division, or to be able to read a novel, or to write a short story with accurate punctuation, spelling and grammar, let alone do *all* of those things. There is a tacit understanding from all involved that some children won't be included in this *all*. When I read *all* I now see *all who matter, all who can be tested, all who we think can be easily measured so we can judge the performance of their school*.

It has yet to come out in the wash, but perhaps the current Secretary of State for Education will take the obvious (but wrong) route out and say that children with statements of SEN won't be included, as happened with the Year 6 SATs resits plan, which was floated just before the 2015 general election. This plan stated that any pupil not securing the government's minimum level of attainment will resit those tests in the first term of Year 7 in their secondary school. Further, the head teachers of those secondary schools will be accountable for their results, with those results published in RAISE-online. Not including children with statements of SEN would exclude many children within that group who are cognitively well developed and keeping up with their peers or, in some cases, well above average. The same would be true if it was decided to filter out just those students attending special schools. Sure, the number still able to achieve this arbitrary line in the sand by the age of 11 would be smaller, but it wouldn't be zero. There is no easy, straightforward solution to this without inadvertently making the statement that the progress of some students matters more than others.

The reason for needing to bring all children up to a certain standard by a certain age is that some children are not achieving this required standard due to poor teaching and poor school leadership – their needs don't mean that they cannot do those things at the age dictated by the government. In the same article *The Sunday Times* reports: 'a future Tory government will remove head teachers who fail to ensure every pupil knows their times tables off by heart.'

In one sentence the landscape for head teachers and leaders in schools that aspire to become more inclusive or to remain inclusive just got tougher. How do you uphold your moral duty as a school leader, and willingly admit students with significant learning difficulties into your Reception or Year 1 classes, or in later year groups if they've left another school, knowing that there is a chance that that particular child will not meet this new required standard? This is not putting a limit on the potential of a child; it is acknowledging that children with some conditions – such as fragile X syndrome (the most common known cause of inherited learning disabilities in this country, by the way, even though you may never have heard of it), Williams syndrome or Down syndrome – will be far less likely to achieve that standard. To be clear, these students may benefit from exceptional teaching, make superb progress and flourish, but they will still be deemed to have failed. Or be discounted.

I'm not sure which is worse. Their achievements count for nothing as the above target has become the sole definition of success.

It's not all; it's all who matter.

This is a clear example of how external pressures can drive the behaviour of head teachers. An example from a parent I spoke to hammers home just how the boundaries of credibility can be stretched in order to ensure as many children as possible are on the right side of the line at the right time:

> I know that in my child's school internal assessments were systematically distorted and inflated to give the impression of outstanding progress over time.
>
> When my child left primary, their internally assessed SATs score showed an age-appropriate NC Level 4 reading. The standardised independent assessments we had commissioned for the Special Educational Needs and Disability Tribunal (SENDIST) told us that they had a reading age of about 6, and the functional grammar of a preschooler. These independent results were corroborated by assessments done at my child's special school at the start of Year 7.

How do you make the correct moral decision to admit a child to your school knowing that it increases the chance of you losing your job? How do you fight against the urge to nudge children up the ladder of whatever assessment system you devise in the absence of levels? How do you fight the urge to then request a change of placement before the child sits a standardised test and makes a mockery of the progress seen previously? If that sounds too cynical, it's because I'm thinking of Jarrod, who came to us at the end of Year 9, apparently working at Level 6 of the national curriculum for English, but barely able to write his own name. I'm thinking of Anthony in Year 11, whose papers arrived on my desk right at the start of the 2015 academic year. He was in a mainstream secondary school for four years *without* an EHCP, then, as soon as an EHCP was granted, with the paper still warm from the printer, the decision was made that he no longer belonged in a secondary school but required specialist provision for the last eight months of his statutory education. I foresee a sequel to the Office of the Children's Commissioner's *'It might be best if you looked elsewhere'* report.

For three years I was fortunate to have the then Secretary of State for Education as my local member of parliament. Michael Gove used to meet with his constituency head teachers termly and this provided us with an ideal opportunity to sit round the table and air issues that were of particular concern. I was always keenly aware that there would come a time when our local MP was not the Secretary of State for Education, so these opportunities were not to be missed.

I initially thought that these meetings would be anodyne affairs as we had to submit questions a week in advance. I imagined a question being read and then Mr Gove giving some kind of ultra-polished answer that had been prepared by a researcher. In fairness to him, Mr Gove always took part in energetic back-and-forth debate, and supplementary questions would fire in from all corners of the meeting room.

Our first meeting occurred around the time of the launch of the Year 1 phonics screening check. There was, and remains, significant concern surrounding this check – and not just from teachers, SENCos, leaders and parents of children with learning difficulties. The concerns surrounding the reasons for these checks have been well documented by Greg Brooks, Emeritus Professor of Education at the University of Sheffield.[3] He notes that:

> No such test can fulfil the avowed purpose of 'a progress check' 'telling parents what they want to know, namely how their children are reading' because
>
> - decoding is only one part of learning to read, and is not reading itself
> - there is no evidence that parents want such a test
> - measuring progress requires at least two tests separated by a suitable interval.
>
> The proposed test commit what has been appropriately called 'the fallacy of the unique methodological solution' – that is, succumbing to the belief that 'if only we can fix this aspect and make all teachers do this particular thing, all (educational, literacy, ...) problems will be solved.'

Those criticisms are system-wide. My particular concern surrounded the evidence for the ways that children with learning difficulties learn to read – not decode. Read. Research findings suggest that phonological awareness in children with Down syndrome is only weakly associated with learning to read.[4] They tend to be more successful using a logographic approach: that is, a whole-word sight recognition approach (i.e. recognising a word such as 'Christmas' in its entirety, and not building up the individual sounds into a whole word) but, importantly, they should practise improving their phonics skills as well, and I brought this to Mr Gove's attention. I explained that this check could artificially label some children as poor readers and, therefore, failures. His response was that he was fully aware of this, but that a measure was required and this was the best option. In this case, the policy was developed in the full knowledge that some students' progress in reading would be excluded or distorted, but this was considered acceptable.

It is another example of the (in this case, phonics-obsessed) tail wagging the dog. We were all told that the Year 1 phonics screening check was simply that – a check. It was not to be used as a performance measure. I presume that explained why it was called a 'check' as opposed to a 'test', and yet the results appear in schools' RAISEonline reports. A colleague explained that her children's school was below the national average last year on this check, and this was part of the reason that Ofsted downgraded the school from its Outstanding grade for the first time.

Jules Daulby, a specialist teacher and assessor of students with specific learning difficulties, has strongly advocated for teachers to take a balanced approach to the teaching of reading. She said that 'no one denies phonics is vital, but this [the screening check] has distorted teaching beyond all recognition'. Jules has written a very good account of her concerns,[5] noting that:

> The check is supposed to be a screener to seek these children out. It is not a diagnostic tool to find out why decoding is difficult. Once we work out who is not a 'reader' from the check, support can be put in place. Early intervention is key, the DfE say, so the check identifies indiscriminately, with no concerns for the why, the children who need this help. If the check highlights difficulties (by that, I mean fail to sound out more than 32-ish out of 40) it is repeated in Year 2 to see if they still have problems decoding words and, as of next year, the proposal is to repeat this check in Year 3.

> The argument from SSP [systematic synthetic phonics] advocates is that 20% of adults in the UK are functionally illiterate – the check, they say, will prevent any child being unable to read. That reading changes lives – we would be mad not to agree, of course. My experience, however, is that it is the few, not the many, who require support, and these needs should be personalised; listening to a child reading diagnostically will capture this. Analytic phonics may be required alongside SSP, for instance, or work on vocabulary might be important. Do they have memory difficulties? Poor phonological awareness? Slow processing speed?

In January 2015 the Minister for Schools, Nick Gibb, said that schools aren't held to account in the phonics screening test, yet the DfE's own website[6] states that the results can be used as a performance measure: 'Ofsted will have access to school-level results via the RAISEonline website for use in inspections. They will use the check results alongside other information about a school's teaching when considering a school's performance.'

The message once again is loud and clear. The evidence is out there regarding the most effective ways to help children with learning difficulties read, but the nuance, the flexibility, the ability to respond, is ignored in favour of the heaviest form of promotion for the preferred method – which, admittedly, is successful for many, but not in isolation. The child with Down syndrome who makes excellent progress with sight recognition of whole words and uses phonics as well, but who may not read most or all 20 nonsense words because he or she doesn't recognise them will fail. And fail again in the resit in Year 2. And fail again in Year 3 if they live in an area conducting this as a pilot. You would have to be a strong head teacher, teacher or SENCo to ignore the looming presence of the screening check and persist with the methods you knew worked best for a child at the expense of trying to hammer away at nonsense words with a child who made swifter progress using a blended approach.

The scrapping of national curriculum levels, announced in 2013, was another example of the failure to consider 100% of children when formulating policy. National curriculum levels supposedly no longer exist, although they are still in use, but P scales remain unaltered.[7]

It may well be that the policy-makers were oblivious to the existence of P scales until it was too late, or that they appreciated this framework couldn't be replaced with a set of end-of-year expectations and standardised tests at certain ages. The decision, if that's what it was, to delay any work on P scales is indicative of the second-class status of the children – and there are thousands – who are at a level of development covered by the P scales.

It took until June 2015 for the government to announce a review of assessment of pupils with, to use their label, lower attainment. To be clear, this is not a review of the P scales. The text of the announcement makes it clear where the government priorities lie:[8]

It is estimated that there are more than 50,000 pupils whose ability falls below the standard required to take national curriculum tests. The review will consider how best to assess the attainment and progress of this group of pupils so that parents know how their children are doing and schools can be given appropriate credit for the work they do to support their pupils.

There are two things that jump out immediately:

- A driver for this review is the concern that arises from the fact that the students do not sit national curriculum tests. There must be some dissatisfaction with the current arrangements for assessing the progress of these students. This dissatisfaction must be rooted in evidence that contradicts, or at least casts serious doubt, on Ofsted's judgement of the progress that students with learning difficulties are making. (Note that, while the special school population and the 50,000 quoted above (that must surely be 50,000 per year) are not precisely the same set of children, there will be some significant overlap.) Ofsted's view is that achievement of pupils is Outstanding in 36% of all special schools and at least Good in 92%.

- Given this statistic, I find the second sentence rather puzzling. The implication is that parents need a clearer system to understand their child's progress. This should be welcomed, but the ambition to give schools appropriate credit for the work they do implies that this is currently absent. Ofsted judgements, whether you like it or not, are the only indicator of quality that counts beyond the school gate.

It is worth noting at this point that the government tried half-heartedly to put together a database of the attainment of all children working at 'below age-related expectations' (their words again) in 2010. It was designed to help schools ensure their targets were aspirational enough and allow parents to gauge their child's progress against all others nationally at the same age and level of attainment.

I say 'half-heartedly', as we were promised an annual consolidation of the datasets to improve the statistical validity of the datasets, which were small to start with, and remain so as the updates never happened. The dataset is also statistically shaky at best, with the smaller cohorts containing sample sizes in the teens. The dataset is also badly contaminated by a population of children with English as an additional language. They appear with low levels of attainment in English, acquire the language skills quickly, and then make rapid progress up the P scales and into the national curriculum levels. This skews the cohort they appear in.

In the same press release mentioned earlier, Minister for Schools Nick Gibb, said:

> Parents of pupils of all abilities have the right to know how their children are progressing at school. My concern is that too many pupils have been at risk of falling into a gap created by a lack of comprehensive assessment for pupils with lower levels of attainment.
>
> This review will help establish accurate information which they can use to hold their school to account. Crucially, it will also give credit to hardworking teachers who rightly have high expectations for all their pupils.

In four sentences, Mr Gibb has cast doubt on the current assessment of children with lower levels of attainment, and seemed to imply that schools with these children in are not currently held to account. My experiences of Ofsted (see Chapter 4) felt very much like being held to account.

I wait with bated breath to see what transpires.

In January 2012 Michael Gove cut the value of over 3,100 vocational qualifications in school league tables in an attempt to stop 'inflated league table rankings'.[9] There may well have been large-scale gaming in order to influence league table positions (the incentives that drive the behaviour of head teachers in schools has been well argued previously): however, the academic good/vocational bad message was clear. I am fortunate to have a very intelligent parent population, and they are utterly convinced of the critical role of vocational education for children with learning difficulties. The statistics for these children, their life chances wrapped up in some dire numbers, were noted in the 'What am I?' section of the introduction. With less than 10% of adults with learning difficulties in work, and the majority of them only working part-time, only a fool or a head teacher under enormous pressure would exclude this crucial area of learning from their curriculum. The message from on high, though, is again clear. These are poor, second-class qualifications compared to academic equivalents.

I've heard the arguments rehearsed many times. The best thing you can do for a child is to give them a solid, high-quality, broad academic education. The children I am concerned about need as much explicit help as we can give them to be able to thrive in society, and to be able to live and work independently. This was something I took for granted when I worked in a mainstream school, but it is far from certain that many young people with learning difficulties will manage this. Not everyone is a fully fledged walker, talker, reader and writer. This is why schools such as my own have a vocational and careers curriculum in school, make use of local further education colleges to support transition, and ensure that all our Year 11 students spend at least a month on work placements. I know many secondary schools are cutting back on their work experience programmes, which seem to be one-week placements, or they have them in half-terms. The twin pressures of shrinking budgets and a focus on exam performance make work experience vulnerable. We must make the investment in our curriculum time to ensure that our students learn as much as they can from time spent in the workplace. There is a significant benefit to this, as employers learn a great deal from our students, and their expectations of young people with learning difficulties are almost always much improved.

Some other brief examples of recent political decision-making that have led to the sense of children with learning difficulties belonging to an underclass:

In June 2013 Michael Gove announced changes to GCSEs and A levels in which modular courses were to be dropped and instead terminal exams would be taken at the end of two years of study. Controlled assessments (i.e. coursework done under exam conditions) were also to be scrapped. You can see how this may affect the ability of some young people, who may be academically very able, but who may find exam conditions intolerable, to give their best. There are many young people with learning difficulties who have strengths in particular subjects but who may struggle with terminal written exams.

From 2016 the government has used a performance measure, Progress 8, which is designed to be more inclusive and capture the achievements of all students. In *Progress 8 measure in 2016, 2017, and 2018*,[10] the DfE states that:

> The Progress 8 measure is designed to encourage schools to offer a broad and balanced curriculum at KS4, and reward schools for the teaching of all their pupils. The new measure will be based on students' progress measured across eight subjects: English; mathematics; three

other English Baccalaureate (EBacc) subjects (sciences, computer science, geography, history and languages); and three further subjects, which can be from the range of EBacc subjects, or can be any other approved, high-value arts, academic, or vocational qualification.

So far, so good. They've even allowed vocational qualifications in there. However, they've recently tinkered with the points that they will assign to the new points score scale for legacy GCSEs – see the table below from the same document.

GCSE grade	2016 Points	2017 Points
G	1.00	1.00
F	2.00	1.50
E	3.00	2.00
D	4.00	3.00
C	5.00	4.00
B	6.00	5.50
A	7.00	7.00
A*	8.00	8.50

Note that the points differentials are not even, and more credit seems to be awarded for upward movement between grades at the top end of the scale than at the bottom, which seems iniquitous.

Prior to the 2015 general election, the Conservative party announced that it would make children who did not reach the expected standard by the end of Year 6 in reading, writing and mathematics resit SATs tests within their first year of secondary school, with the numbers of children who failed the resits being published in the league table data.[11] In 2014, 79% of Year 6 children reached the expected standard. It was interesting to read that, this time round, the government proactively announced that children 'with special needs' would not have to take the resits. Again, there may well be children within that group who could have reached or exceeded the required benchmark but, for any number of reasons, it was deemed (this time, in a positive way for the children concerned) best to omit them from the requirements of the policy.

What could we do to influence policy to allow for nuance, difference and context?

• As a profession, we should collectively refuse to join in with the game that the government want us to play with its attempts to influence our behaviour with policy diktats. The EBacc is a case in point. Nicky Morgan announced in June 2015 that this suite of qualifications would be compulsory for all students beginning Year 7 in September 2015 to study at GCSE level. *SecEd* (http://www. sec-ed.co.uk/) reported on a study of 1,300 school leaders which indicated that many schools currently judged to be Outstanding by Ofsted will refuse to make the EBacc compulsory – a decision that means the ceiling for future Ofsted judgements for that school will be set at Good (45% of respondents from Outstanding schools said that they would refuse to implement the compulsory EBacc even if it meant losing their Outstanding status).[12] Sir Michael Wilshaw, Her Majesty's Chief Inspector of Schools, characteristically waded in to the debate in an interview with the *TES*, saying that he could 'think of youngsters who would have been better suited to do English, maths and science and a range of vocational subjects.'[13]

Nicky Morgan said in November 2015 to think tank Policy Exchange that: 'I think every child should study maths, English, history or geography, a language and the sciences up until the age of 16.'[14] I don't. Head teachers need to show real leadership here and ensure the curriculum in their school is organised to the best advantage of the students who are in it. I am with Sir Michael Wilshaw on this one, and I'm sure there are many more head teachers out there who feel the same way.

It is interesting to note that Nicky Morgan's position had changed in the five months between the policy announcement (when she said, to quote the *TES* article, 'that making the EBacc compulsory for all was a matter of "social justice"') and the November 2015 consultation, which states the aim that 90% of students in mainstream secondary schools will be entered for the EBacc, with special schools and alternative provisions not expected to meet the 90% ambition. The government either believes that this suite of qualifications is transformative in terms of social mobility, as indicated by the use of the term 'social justice', or it doesn't. If it does, then surely it should be compulsory for those who fare least well in terms of social mobility now? It is precisely this group who are omitted in the 90% aim stated above.

- I am drawn to the proposal by Dr Becky Allen, Director of Education Datalab, that school league tables should be weighted to reflect situational factors such as late arrivals and time spent at each school. This would go a long way towards reflecting the context of many of our schools, particularly those schools that are net recipients of pupils out of the normal calendar of admissions, especially as external tests and exams approach. As stated above, at the end of 2015, approximately 25% of the students at my school had been to a mainstream secondary school and had to leave, usually because of their behaviour. Some left in Year 7 (one after six days, but not due to his behaviour, to be clear), but more left from older year groups. Students move school for many reasons but some sharing of credit or risk, difficult as it would be to fairly apportion, would seem equitable.

Notes

1. A. Clark, *Alan Clark Diaries: In Power 1983–1992* (London: Weidenfeld & Nicolson, 1993), p. 26.
2. See http://www.thesundaytimes.co.uk/sto/news/article1513958. ece?CMP=OTH-gnws-standard-2015_01_31.
3. See https://ukla.org/news/story/ professor_greg_brooks_critiques_the_governments_proposed_decoding_test_for.
4. See http://www.down-syndrome.org/reviews/2066/.
5. See https://mainstreamsen.wordpress.com/2015/04/01/ mother-courage-of-the-reading-wars/.
6. See https://www.gov.uk/government/publications/ key-stage-1-assessment-and-reporting-arrangements-ara/phonics-screening-check#how-results-will-be-used-by-the-department-for-education-and-ofsted.
7. The P scales are the extrapolation of national curriculum levels for use in assessing children who are judged to be working below Level 1, and they range from P1i to P8.
8. See https://www.gov.uk/government/news/ special-needs-expert-to-head-new-assessment-review.
9. See http://www.bbc.co.uk/news/education-16808902.
10. See https://www.gov.uk/government/uploads/system/uploads/attachment_data/ file/415486/Progress_8_school_performance_measure.pdf, p. 5.
11. See http://www.bbc.co.uk/news/education-32204578.
12. See http://www.sec-ed.co.uk/news/ schools-willing-to-sacrifice-outstanding-grade-over-ebacc.
13. See https://www.tes.com/news/school-news/breaking-news/ wilshaw-and-dfe-ebac-collision-course.
14. See https://www.gov.uk/government/speeches/nicky-morgan-one-nation-education.

Chapter 7

Driving Without Brakes

'I believe that every act of violence is also a message that needs to be understood.'

Jean Vanier, *Becoming Human*

Michael was the perfect stereotype for the tabloids to hate. The son of a man who had been in prison for possession of Class A drugs (crack cocaine, in his case), with intent to supply; the son of a mother who was a drug user; the nephew of a man in prison for supplying Class A drugs; a boy surrounded by adult relatives who hadn't had a paid job for many years; a boy already permanently excluded from a special school for violence towards adults and other children; a boy already involved in the criminal justice system at the age of 14 for regularly committing thefts from motor vehicles. Michael is also black. As you can imagine, the statistics that exist for all of us indicating life expectancy, employment prospects, wealth, and the like were dire for Michael.

Michael remains one of the two or three most difficult young people I've ever taught, and I loved teaching him and working with him. I vividly remember Michael's first day at our school in Slough for children with social, emotional and behavioural difficulties. The police were called as Michael had broken the window of our minibus with a stone. I remember the time he tried to get in to my science lesson via the fire exit using a scaffold pole as a battering ram. It was unconventional, but I took heart from the fact that he was trying to enter my lesson rather than leave it. I've never met someone who had such a finely tuned defensive radar. It was always in active mode, sweeping the vicinity for signs of anything unidentified that would immediately be labelled as a THREAT. For Michael, figures of authority were categorised as a THREAT; posh teachers (his words, sanitised) were definitely categorised as a THREAT; anyone he judged to be from a different social class was a clear THREAT.

When confronted with someone he judged to be dangerous, Michael had developed a very successful strategy of getting the first punch in, metaphorically speaking. I observed him successfully render a colleague completely powerless once, despite my best efforts and those of another colleague, by persistent, aggressive questioning, interruption, intimidation and mild threats of physical violence. Mission accomplished – no work done.

I worked with Michael for nearly two years, teaching him science but also trying to get to know him as well as I could and trying to build some trust into our relationship. I only ever managed one conversation with him of any real lucidity and of any real duration in that time, and it will remain with me forever. I was asked to remove Michael from a lesson where he was persistently threatening a teacher, and I managed to get him to open up to me. Think unmet needs here. Michael was successful in his quest to be removed from his lesson, so in order to prevent a return (which I would not have done in any case, given the circumstances, but he didn't know this) and to avoid doing any written work it was in his best interests to talk to me.

We talked about the future. Knowing how desperate his home circumstances were, I was interested to know where his thoughts lay. (I deliberately avoided using the word 'ambition' there, as I am convinced that Michael had nothing approaching an ambition, sadly.) At that point Michael was stealing portable satellite navigation systems from cars at night on a regular basis. You could tell when he had been out late as he would be very sleepy the next day, either from lack of sleep or because he'd been in custody the night before. Regardless, he'd be in school the next day.

'Morning, Michael.'

'TomTom, innit,' would be his curt reply, indicating that he'd been out on the hunt the night before. It never ceased to amaze me that he regarded the fact that he stole bikes in order to transport himself around as no problem. 'I don't keep 'em, Mr O'B!'

It took some prompting, but Michael indicated an interest in working in landscape gardening as he loved being outdoors, liked using hand tools, creating things and nature. We talked through all the steps he would need to go through to achieve this. Michael, despite his difficulties, had a quick brain – he needed one to try to stay one step ahead of the police at night. He was streetwise and he knew all the things he needed to do to achieve his goal. Michael knew he would need some GCSEs passes at Level 1 to secure a place at a further education college on a Level 2 course. This meant working to accept the support on offer at our school and increasing his workload and commitment. He knew he would have to attend the college for an interview, smartly dressed, and complete a written application. He knew that we would support him writing the application form and could help with the interview preparation, but that he would have to answer the questions himself. He knew that if he secured a place on the course, and then was successful, he would have to complete job application forms and attend job interviews to secure a job. Michael knew that we, and others, would support him at each step of the process, but ultimately he would have to do the work.

It boiled down to two facts:

- Michael knew the odds of failure at each step were higher than he was prepared to accept, so he wouldn't commit. Not to any of the steps, let alone the entire process.

- Michael was well respected by the people that mattered to him for his current 'job' and he made good money doing it, the illegality of it being in no way a deterrent (in fact, it may have been a badge of honour). Michael never admitted whether or not he liked his life. He may well have done, although I have my suspicions.

The scale of the challenge facing those of us who cared about Michael was daunting. It would take something monumental to change Michael's view that he should do anything other than what he was very success-fully doing now. I was also painfully aware that I was imposing my own expectations onto him of what I believe constitutes a successful working adult life: that is, one where you legitimately work, if you are able, and pay taxes. It was far from certain that Michael shared this view. Michael shows why recidivism rates remain high. For him, reoffending was far more preferable to any other alternative. He enjoyed stealing and, as an added bonus, he got a kick out of evading the police, whom he despised. (Keeping from Michael and a number of other students the fact that I was a serving Special Constable was one of my biggest challenges at that school.)

Michael ended our conversation in a manner designed to make me realise that he didn't really care after all – 'You're chattin' shit, Mr O'B' – and with that he walked off to his next lesson.

I'd like this story to have a happy ending, but alas …

I left the school before Michael did, but less than three minutes searching the internet tells me that in January 2014, Michael, of no fixed abode (one of the most depressing phrases I know), was convicted of robbery and then, later, jailed for 18 months for assault occasioning actual bodily harm. I'm deeply saddened, but not surprised.

The significant known over-representation of both children and adults with learning difficulties in the criminal justice system is the tip of an iceberg that has persisted for many years with little sign of decreasing. In 2012, the Annual Report of the Chief Medical Officer noted specifically about children in the criminal justice system that 'Over a quarter of children and young people in the youth justice system have a learning disability. Some 60% of boys in custody have specific difficulties in relation to speech, language or communication.'[1] (Think back to Lindsay and Dockrell's 2010 report in Chapter 2 on the relationship between speech, language and communication needs and behavioural, emotional and social difficulties.)

The Prison Reform Trust produced a very informative report that laid bare the scale of the problem for children and adults. I've summarised the findings here:[2]

- between a fifth and a third of offenders have learning difficulties that impair their ability to cope with the demands of the criminal justice system;

- this group are at risk of reoffending because their needs may not have been correctly identified or, indeed, identified at all and this could result in a consequent lack of support and access to services;

- they are unlikely to benefit from conventional programmes to address offending behaviours, precisely because these programmes are less likely to take into consideration their specific needs;

- these offenders are prone to being targeted by other prisoners;

- the staff who work with them often lack specialist training or are unfamiliar with the challenges of working with this offenders with learning difficulties.

One of the major common underlying issues is functional illiteracy. This is unsurprising, but the sheer prevalence and level of literacy difficulties are disturbing. The report noted that prison-based studies seem to settle on a figure of approximately 30% for the proportion of prisoners with dyslexia and 'rates of serious deficits in literacy and numeracy [generally considered to be abilities below the age of an 11-year-old] in general reach up to 60%.'[3] This comes from research conducted by Herrington (2005)[4] who reported that the Basic Skills Agency Initial Assessment found that 60% of prisoners had a reading ability equivalent to, or less than, that of a five-year-old child.

The information is patchy. Very little is known about the prevalence of learning difficulties among women, but what is known points towards a higher rate than for men or children (at about 40%), and among ethnic groups the information is described as 'virtually non-existent.'[5]

Given the scale of representation described above, it would seem at first glance that children, and in this case adults, with learning difficulties are far from invisible in the criminal justice system. However, the true number of people is not known, as many of the needs are either not identified for a long period of time, or remain hidden. This is unsurprising as The Prison Reform Trust found that:

> Equally problematic is the identification of needs without having the facilities to address them. Prison staff expressed a need for training and for defined policies about how to address the needs of people with learning disabilities or learning difficulties. (N. Loucks, *No One Knows*, p. 3)

In addition to identification (and it is encouraging to see prison staff actively seeking to learn about how best to support these people), where needs are known about many other issues remain.

The use of community-based orders to manage the behaviour and conduct of offenders outside of prison poses an issue for individuals who have learning difficulties and/or autistic spectrum disorders and are placed under such orders. The charity the British Institute for Brain Injured Children (BIBIC) launched a campaign in 2005 called 'Ain't

Misbehavin' to voice their concerns that a disproportionate number of community-based orders, then called Anti-Social Behaviour Orders (ASBO), were imposed on children or young people with learning difficulties, ADHD or other behavioural difficulties.[6]

It can be seen that children or young people with learning difficulties or autistic spectrum disorders may find it challenging to understand the terms of an order or why it has been imposed. It follows then, that compliance with the terms of such community-based orders will be less likely, which then increases the chances of the young person ending up in prison: precisely the thing community-based orders were designed to avoid in the first place.

The regime, rules and routines in young offender institutions and prisons can also be difficult for people with learning difficulties to get used to. The arising frustrations can lead to an increase in negative behaviours (think unmet needs here), such as those detailed in the *No One Knows* report. The report found that negative or disruptive behaviours, such as the inappropriate use of emergency alarms in cells, shouting, kicking doors and damage to property, were linked to the learning difficulties of some prisoners. It also found that such behaviours could result in these prisoners being targeted by other prisoners.

Worryingly the report found that some prisoners with learning difficulties were not able to take part in offender behaviour programmes because of their difficulties. I assert that they are precisely the group who are in most need of such programmes. It should be of no surprise then that the report found that frustration at being excluded from these programmes led to prisoners sometimes becoming violent or isolating themselves, or, more worryingly, being isolated by the prison staff for their own protection. This isolation, self-imposed or enforced, only increases 'their vulnerability to problems such as mental distress and suicide'.[7]

It seems self-defeating to set up a system of rehabilitation and then exclude precisely the group of offenders who is in greatest need of that support. I am reminded of the pupil referral unit (PRU) that perversely refused to take children from mainstream schools unless their behaviour improved to the extent that they felt the child had 'earned' (their word) their place at the PRU.

Children in the criminal justice system, like Michael, often become men and women in the criminal justice system and, as we saw above, that is precisely what Michael became. Working with them can sometimes feel futile – and it is difficult not to feel a sense of futility right now as I write this, knowing how Michael's life has evolved to date. If we are to do anything other than shake our heads mournfully at the state of things, then we need to recognise that the statistics above represent an accumulation of problems that can lead to recidivism. The alternatives are unattractive, the problems entrenched, the functional illiteracy dominating every facet of their life, but remaining unseen to many. This is why it is vital that those of us who work with children who may be at risk of ending up in the criminal justice system or who are already along that slippery slope recognise that basic literacy and numeracy skills and good speech, language and communication development are life-changers for teenagers who resist learning, sometimes in aggressive and violent ways. They can be some of the hardest young people to teach, but they need us to turn up day after day with the same determination and commitment, and always with one eye on what their future could be like if we succeed.

What can the teaching profession do to ensure children with special needs do not end up on the wrong side of the criminal justice system?

- Once children and young adults are in the criminal justice system, the work we are able to do is, frankly, of limited value. We have absolutely no idea if, years from now, the young people we work with who have a background such as Michael's will end up in the criminal justice system, but we must recognise that there are things we can do to reduce the chances of this happening. While young people are still in our schools, we must continue to do our absolute best to ensure they leave us in the best shape possible, even if they have begun to travel down a road that it's hard to return from. This means ensuring their curriculum is relevant. The EBacc is not the best possible curriculum offer for *every* young person at Key Stage 4 and the current lack of political enthusiasm for vocational study before the age of 16 does not, in my view, encourage schools to do this to the extent that is needed. The shocking rates of illiteracy noted above also point to a need for the greater use of functional English courses and qualifications at Key Stage 4, perhaps at the expense of, dare I say it at the risk of offending purists, English literature or modern foreign languages.

- I stated my views in Chapter 2 that sanctions and punishments are largely ineffective in improving the behaviour of children with learning difficulties. This reliance on extrinsic motivation – the carrot and stick of reward and punishment – means we potentially pay less attention to developing intrinsic motivation – doing the right thing simply because it is the right thing to do. When I provide training on behaviour I often use speeding as an example to highlight this point. We don't want motorists to exceed the speed limit for obvious reasons. Lawmakers, advised by persons suitably qualified, make decisions about the maximum speed we are permitted to drive in any given area. Ideally we would see all motorists respectfully observe speed limits out of respect for the law and an understanding that speeding increases the risk of harm to both the driver and others around them – doing the right thing because it's the right thing to do. Despite this, some motorists speed regularly and with impunity, hence the need for speeding fines, points sanctions on driving licences and offences such as 'driving without due care and attention'. Fortunately the law recognises that there are other ways to improve driver behaviour, which is why speed awareness courses are sometimes used as alternatives in an attempt to impress upon drivers the effects of their actions on others. This is consistent with the principles of restorative practice which focuses on: repair (crime causes harm and this needs to be repaired); the parties deciding together how this is to be done; and by doing so aiming to provoke positive changes in people and their relationships. Alfie Kohn's *Beyond Discipline* is an excellent resource for more on intrinsic motivation. He argues: 'Punishment does absolutely nothing to promote [knowing how one ought to act and being concerned about others]. In fact, it tends to undermine good values by fostering a preoccupation with self-interest'.[8] If we think again about Michael above – his main concern was not the effect of his actions on others; rather, it was the selfish need to avoid being caught. In order to do that, he needed to improve his skills as a criminal, not desist from such behaviour.

- It is vital that teachers know that a relationship exists between speech, language and communication needs and behavioural, emotional and social difficulties. Once we establish that a child has language difficulties, there are practical things that those of us in schools can do, often with the support of a speech and language therapist. Given the media reports of the numbers of young children starting school with delayed acquisition of language skills, this is crucial. The 2012 Annual Report of the Chief Medical Officer revealed that some '60% of boys in custody have specific difficulties in relation to speech, language or communication', as discussed previously. Improving the speech, language and communication skills of children as soon as possible would seem therefore to be a good protective factor improving the chances of some of those young children ending up in the criminal justice system later on.

Notes

1. C. Lennox and L. Khan, 'Youth justice'. In *Our Children Deserve Better: Prevention Pays*, the Annual Report of the Chief Medical Officer 2012 (2012). Available at: https://www.gov.uk/government/uploads/system/uploads/attachment_data/file/252662/33571_2901304_CMO_Chapter_12.pdf, p. 2.
2. N. Loucks, *No One Knows – offenders with learning difficulties and learning disabilities – review of prevalence and associated needs*. Prison Reform Trust, 2007. Available at: http://www.ohrn.nhs.uk/resource/policy/NoOneKnowPrevalence.pdf, p. 1.
3. Loucks, *No One Knows*, p. 2.
4. V. Herrington, 'Meeting the healthcare needs of offenders with learning disabilities'. *Learning Disability Practice* (2005), 8(4): 28–32.
5. Loucks, *No One Knows*, p. 2.
6. See A. Flannagan, 'Tarred with the same brush', *The Guardian* (8 May 2006). Available at: http://www.theguardian.com/uk/2006/may/08/ukcrime.immigrationpolicy.
7. Loucks, *No One Knows*, p. 2.
8. A. Kohn, *Beyond Discipline: From compliance to community* (Alexandria, VA: Association for Supervision and Curriculum Development, 1996), p. 29.

Chapter 8

A Relief Map of the Himalayas

'It doesn't make a difference how beautiful your guess is, it doesn't make a difference how smart you are, who made the guess or what his name is. If it disagrees with experiment, it is wrong.'

Richard Feynman (1918–1988), Nobel prize-winning physicist

In the world of SEN there is no more emotive word, and no word that will provoke greater entrenchment, than the word 'inclusion'– the principle that all children should be taught well in their local mainstream school and have their needs met there. It's a word with as many vociferous opponents as proponents.

The strongest proponents maintain the view that inclusion is right in principle, irrespective of the quality of the education a child may receive. The act of including a child far outweighs any drawbacks that the inclusion may bring. The fact that the child may make far better academic and social progress in a specialist school is considered to be less important than the fact the child is with their peers. This is a child's basic right, they will argue, and to say anything different is to deny that child at least some part of their entitlement.

Inclusion of all children is not something that I believe is possible. It is not possible, because there are some children whose needs are so complex, who require such specialist skill and knowledge from professionals, who may require specialist equipment and who exhibit such extreme behaviours that they cannot be meaningfully included and well educated in a mainstream school. To pretend to include them in the life of such a school is far more damaging – and, in my view, robs them of their entitlement.

The strongest opponents to inclusion argue that placing children with SEN in classes with children within the normal cognitive ability range has too great an impact on teachers, the school's budget and other students, regardless of the fact that the child may be making exceptional progress.

Neither of these interest groups finds much satisfaction with the current state of England's education system. To those far removed from the business end of teaching, 'inclusion' represents an infinitesimally thin, neat line. On one side of this straight line are children who are educated in mainstream schools. On the other side of the line are children who are educated in special schools because their educational and associated health needs are so complex that they would, in all likelihood, fail to thrive in mainstream schools.

In reality the line is not straight, nor is it thin. It is porous and is criss-crossed by other delineations – the education of children in separate boys' and girls' schools; the education of children in schools defined by a religious affiliation; the education of children in schools defined by academic selection (and others with the added criteria of the ability to pay). Given that many schools hold more than one of these designations, including some special schools which have a religious affiliation, the line instead looks like a bowl of spaghetti or a relief map of the Himalayas.

As a nation we don't take exception to single-sex schools – we regard it as perfectly normal for parents to choose to send their children to schools where near on 50% of the population is missing. We do not regard this form of segregation as a removal of a fundamental right of those children. It is not forced segregation; it is a positive choice in most cases. No politician will ever remove single-sex schools in England. They are ingrained into our national psyche in an 'I went to an all-boys school and it never did me any harm' manner.

However, we do not enjoy such unanimity in our views of schools that are described as Roman Catholic, Church of England, Sikh, Hindu or Muslim. Many people believe that organised religion should have nothing to do with running schools. The political fallout from the Trojan Horse affair in Birmingham (a plot to oust some Birmingham head teachers and make their schools adhere to more Islamic principles) and the subsequent push by the government to promote British Values highlighted how an adherence to some religious principles can override the fundamental need to offer a broad and balanced curriculum.

126

Objections raised against state schools that select by ability tend to be on the grounds that they inhibit social mobility by being full of middle-class children. I reject the notion that grammar schools produced accountants who would otherwise have become bricklayers, meaning that we need more such schools that select by ability. Objections to private schools that select by ability and on parents' ability to pay again rest on concerns about social segregation and the protection of privilege. This is considered a benefit to some; one friend candidly told me: 'My kids will go private as I can't have them mixing with certain other types of kids.'

What does the research say?

Where objections remain, they are principled objections. So, what evidence is there that inclusive schools (defined as mainstream schools with higher proportions of children with SEN) do better – or worse – by their children? Dyson et al. (2004)[1] comprehensively researched this for the then Department for Education and Skills, and their findings were very interesting.

At the level of the local authority there was no evidence of a relationship between attainment and levels of inclusion (reflected in the proportion of pupils educated in mainstream schools) when other variables are taken into consideration.

At the level of the individual school they found a 'very small and negative statistical relationship' between the school's level of inclusion and the attainment of its pupils. They consider it unlikely that this relationship is a causal one for a number of reasons. Schools that were similar in terms of inclusivity varied widely in their performance, suggesting other factors were at play. Schools that were more inclusive tended to also serve a more disadvantaged population, which is also correlated with lower attainment. The observable differences seemed to have more to do with factors not directly attributable to inclusion such as resources, staff skill levels and methods of implementation.

Interestingly, they noted a positive view of inclusion from teachers and pupils, who observed the positive effects on the wider achievements of all pupils. Lastly, they note, importantly, that their 'findings are in line with the international research evidence. Most studies find few if any negative impacts of inclusion on the attainments and achievements of pupils without SEN.'[2]

We are all naturally drawn towards evidence that supports our cognitive biases, and there is certainly something in the above findings for most people to cherry-pick from to bolster their position, but there is nothing to support the views of those at the poles of the continuum of opinion.

That there needs to be specialist provision for some children is indisputable, and as such full inclusion is impossible. I have yet to see a school that is fully inclusive. Some schools are very inclusive and others are less inclusive. The real debate centres on policies and practices that schools implement, both deliberately and inadvertently, that work against children with learning difficulties, disabilities and other forms of special educational need.

The stratified system in England

The school that I serve is very non-inclusive (I hesitate to use the word 'exclusive', to avoid misunderstanding). We are unable to effectively educate the overwhelming majority of children in this country. This is stating the obvious, but some schools seem reluctant to admit that they are non-inclusive, claiming to be fully inclusive for fear of appearing elitist. I counter this, though, with the brazen example of a special school that stated on the home page of its website quite categorically that it didn't admit children with either learning difficulties or behavioural issues. A change of head teacher has, thankfully, seen that statement removed.

In England, 97.2% of school-age children do not require a statement of SEN or EHCP.[3] Of those that do, the majority (55%) are educated in mainstream schools. Interestingly, this picture is variable across the country. In the county in which I work, less than 50% of the children with statements or EHCPs are educated in mainstream schools. Meanwhile, 1.1% of all school-age children in this country are educated in special schools, a statistic that has been relatively stable for many years. This stability is interesting because, at the time of writing, the DfE has issued a report indicating that the numbers of children requiring special school placements will rise by 31% in the next nine years, compared to a 12% rise for the school-age population as a whole.[4] Despite my best efforts I am unable to find out from the DfE how they arrived at such a figure. (Helpfully DfE release background information with lots of their reports and this one is no different, but there is nothing in there explaining such an extrapolation and it is way out of line with projected rises in primary and secondary places.)

I claim to have a wide perspective on schools. I taught science and physics, as well as other subjects, in a comprehensive school for five years. I taught physics and ICT in a selective boys' secondary independent school. I taught maths and science and was the deputy head teacher in a secondary special school for boys with social, emotional and behavioural difficulties. I taught science and communication, language and literacy, and was the deputy head teacher in a large 2–19 special school for children with moderate, severe, profound and multiple learning difficulties or autism. I am now the head teacher of a special school for students aged 11–19 with moderate learning difficulties and associated conditions such as autism and/or Down syndrome. I've taught children who have gone to Oxford and Cambridge University. I've taught children who have gone to prison, either as children or as adults. I've taught children who died young because of their congenital conditions. Each school I have worked in had its own niche. If you work in an educational establishment of any sort, then yours does too. Some establishments admit, accept and include children with a very wide range of needs; others do not. Each school has its own natural limits, and my experience tells me that these are largely set by the leaders of the school. There are children that each school will consider outside its typical range, and it is the leaders in that school who determine how flexible those limits are.

In the comprehensive I first worked in, pupils clearly had to be of a certain age to be admitted – no problem there. Apart from Peter in my tutor group, of course, who was allowed to progress to secondary school a year early on account of his ability. No one seemed exercised by that, despite the fact that he was clearly segregated from the rest of Year 6, who were still hammering away at SATs papers (he dodged that bullet, at least). All the departments set limits, totally independently, it seemed, on who could do A levels: to study any science at A level required a minimum of a grade C at GCSE, but at some point during my time at the school it became policy that you couldn't progress to studying maths at A level with anything less than a B at GCSE. We had a fair number of students with statements (we were considered inclusive locally, and often took children from other schools) but I now know that we did not do a good job of educating most of them. They were included, but not meaningfully, and at a cost to their academic and social development. And they all had moderate learning difficulties, Asperger syndrome or, rarely, Down syndrome. We couldn't possibly have effectively taught a child with severe or complex difficulties. We would have cobbled together some kind of timetable to do our best, but the results would have been poor. Compared to some of our neighbours, we had a very flexible and inclusive attitude, but there was an almost complete lack of technical expertise beyond that required to teach children with moderate learning difficulties. The addition of needs associated with speech and language, physical difficulties or rather more challenging behaviour would have defeated us.

I saw a different set of institutional boundaries when I worked in an independent school. Gender, academic ability and the ability to pay were the deciding factors. Interestingly, gender ceased to become an issue in the sixth form, when we saw fit to admit girls. I presumed this was because we filtered out some boys at the end of Year 11 every year who had relatively disappointing GCSE results and were therefore not considered sixth-form material, so we needed to make up the numbers. The idea that sixth-form boys were more mature and could therefore be relied upon not to be distracted by girls wouldn't have held much water. A child was considered to be at the edge of educability at GCSE grade C level. My next-door neighbour would proudly announce that students below this arbitrary level were unteachable. I'll never forget 'I've just taught two bottom sets in a row. I feel like I don't know how to teach.'

Who can't be meaningfully included?

When you claim to be inclusive, what exactly are you including the students in? How are they being included? What are you trying to teach them? Is the way you are trying to teach the way they learn best? Is this appropriate for their stage of development, while being age-appropriate? The painful recollections from parents in Chapter 5 are a stark reminder of what schools can sometimes do in the mistaken idea that they are being inclusive, when they are being anything but. This is where I see real segregation – the child who is taught exclusively by a teaching assistant all week is effectively in a school of one child. The size of the school that surrounds them is irrelevant and becomes background noise. The child becomes invisible to the rest of the school. This is what leads to the – I hope – occasional teaching assistant referring to children as 'My statement has autism…' 'My Down's statement is…' etc. as I mentioned in Chapter 3.

So who do I claim cannot receive their basic entitlement in their local mainstream school? The students I describe below. They are all real people I have known and taught, who were well educated in special schools. Even with the greatest possible will and with a significant investment in money and resources, I still claim that these students, and many more, would not be well served by being placed in their local mainstream school. I haven't even tried to describe some of the needs of some students in PRUs who have all come from a mainstream school, hospital schools (special schools that provide education for pupils of school age who are unable to attend school for medical or mental health reasons for varying amounts of time and who may well be in-patients in a hospital) or secure children's homes. If you have time, I recommend you read an interview with Richard Albery, who is the SENCo in a secure children's home, to learn more about this vital, but unseen, part of our education estate and the dedicated people who work in them.[5]

If a school is to be fully inclusive, all the staff would need training and the school building would require adaptations. To start with, you'd need piped oxygen, a hydrotherapy pool, hoists, changing beds for children (some of them over six feet tall and the weight of a fully grown man), plus the staff to manage that. You'd need good knowledge of epilepsy, vagus nerve stimulators, diabetes, hearing impairments, visual impairments, sign language and occupational therapy techniques. I could go on. Perhaps you can now see why this 1.1% of the population accounts for about 10% of the education budget.

Shona is a teenager and is profoundly disabled, blind, and breathes through a tracheotomy. She is tube-fed and incontinent. Nearly all interactions with Shona are fully prompted by the adults who work with her. She is considered to be working at P3i. If she was in your Year 9 history lesson, what would you teach her? How? If she was in your primary classroom, how would you ensure that she took part in PE or art? How does Shona even know who you are, or what lesson she is in? How does she get to your classroom on the first floor? How does she catch up on the classwork she misses when she is being fed or changed? How do you enforce the school's rule that all students have their top button done up? Do you even know what P3i means, and would you recognise P3ii when you saw it? If you don't, then who in the school does?

Joe has foetal alcohol syndrome which took years to diagnose because of the stigma attached to it. Joe will usually try to avoid work at all costs because his fear of failure and embarrassment is overwhelming, and he can be violent towards both students and staff. He will normally enter your lesson announcing, 'I ain't doin' any fucking [insert the name of the subject or lesson here] today.' He may rip up his worksheet, exercise book or textbook. He won't have done your homework because the reading age of the text on your worksheet is likely to be far above his own. Joe is likely to leave your lesson at some point, or he may not arrive at all.

Abdul is academically only slightly below the level expected of his age, but has significant physical difficulties and some moderate learning difficulties. Abdul is highly motivated to learn and will try very hard to take a full part in lessons by making noises to secure attention. Other pupils are likely to find his noises irritating. Abdul propels himself in a walking frame, but cannot navigate by himself. Abdul has very poor fine motor skills, cannot pincer-grip well, and his speech is virtually unintelligible. How do you communicate with Abdul? He can follow your work, but how do you assess his progress? How does he catch up on the work he misses when he is at speech therapy? And occupational therapy? And physiotherapy? And being changed? How does he meaningfully take part in your science investigations or PE lessons?

Ross has cerebral palsy and hypertonia – that is, his arms and legs are stiff and difficult to move. He requires intensive physiotherapy and regular Botox injections to reduce his muscle tone and improve his range of motion. Ross communicates via eye-gaze technology, which requires significant time with both Ross and staff to learn how to use it.

In my experience, most head teachers and most class teachers accept that full inclusion is a myth. I applaud those who are committed to meeting a wide range of needs. I see some exceptional practice, and this tends to permeate the whole school and is often driven by a moral conviction and strong leadership. Often the leaders in these schools are developing their inclusive practice in the full knowledge that other schools may secretly be pleased that there is strong local expertise in SEN elsewhere.

It is clear that primary schools are in a better position to be inclusive than secondary schools. The challenge of meeting complex educational and health needs clearly becomes harder the older the children are. Differences and delays in academic and social development are harder to spot in very young children. Children develop communication skills at different rates (remember those conversations you had with other parents in which you compared your child's speech to theirs?), and it can be difficult for parents to decide if a delay in acquiring a skill is a problem or if they just need to wait for another three months before mentioning it to their GP. Children become continent at different rates, too, and I find that this can be one of the first sources of tension with schools. Some schools have a policy of not admitting children into their nursery or reception classes if the child is not continent. This directly discriminates against many children with SEN that are a result of a medical condition. Continence may come many years later, and all the time they are unable to begin formal schooling they are missing vital learning time. Some children learn to regulate their behaviour much earlier than others, and it is not uncommon for young children to struggle emotionally for a while when away from their parents. In Reception or Year 1, there can be many such children. In Year 7, however, they stick out like a sore thumb. It is no surprise, then, to point out that in 2015 the number of children in special schools who are in Year 7 is 40% more than those in Year 6. For parents, realising that their child will have to negotiate a much larger school environment – with, potentially, support from a teaching assistant for all or part of the week – is often a watershed moment.

Primary schools have advantages in other areas too. Usually a child will have one class teacher who can get to know the child and parents well. Face-to-face interaction with their child's class teacher can happen on an almost daily basis, and this can be reassuring for parents. They can be much more satisfied that the teacher understands their child's needs well. Primary schools are much more likely to be single-storey and are usually relatively small. When all of those things disappear at secondary school, this can be the beginning of the end. It is no surprise that, at the time of writing, nearly a quarter of my students initially went to a mainstream secondary school but had to leave as their schools, rightly or wrongly, felt they couldn't meet their needs.

I reject the assertion that any school can be fully inclusive. I am concerned that there are schools who, having mistakenly become slaves to the Ofsted inspection handbook, are becoming less inclusive. The head teacher, now thankfully retired, who stood up at open evening to announce: 'If your child has any form of additional needs, then this is not the school for them'; the head teachers who quietly suggest to prospective parents that they look at the neighbouring school because 'they're better with your kind of child'; or the schools like the one we have already met which describe themselves as 'academic' all contribute to this.

Inclusion joins *outstanding* on the list of tainted, misused and purloined words that those of us in the education profession shouldn't be using any more. I prefer to think of schools as being committed to providing the support to which a child is *entitled*. Entitled, because their needs may well have been enshrined in a document that places a legal obligation on schools to provide what is needed. But it goes deeper than just meeting the legal demands of the statement or EHCP. Schools have a moral and ethical duty to provide that to which each child is entitled. For example, speech and language therapy is not a luxury. It's not an added extra. It has been established by fellow professionals in other fields (whose judgements we should respect) that a child needs support to gain the skills to communicate in a way that the rest of us do without any conscious thought or effort. The same is true for occupational therapy, physiotherapy, hydrotherapy or psychotherapy.

You need to put your own feelings away about whether ADHD or reactive attachment disorder actually exist or not, and focus on meeting the needs that a particular child quite clearly has. To simply put a child's behaviour down to poor parenting is both singularly unhelpful and counter-productive.

It is one thing to accept that there are children whose needs are so complex that it is perfectly reasonable to make specialist provision for them in certain types of school. It is quite another to decide that your school doesn't 'do' SEN because the school is 'academic', that provision detailed in statements or EHCPs is optional, or that children with complex needs must have their breaks and lunchtimes in separate areas.

As I write this chapter, my mind continually wanders back to the same thought. My school offers free bespoke outreach services to local mainstream schools (as do many special schools), funded by our local authority. The schools that ask us for the most support are the ones I know for sure are already thoroughly committed to ensuring that their children get everything to which they are entitled, and that it is of high quality.

They are the Anne Bindings of this world, the woman we met in Chapter 1. They know that they do a good job, but are determined to be even better, and to ensure that they do the best they can for every one of their students. When they admit children they do so on the basis of a firm commitment. If they say yes, they mean it for the duration. They don't have a 'let's give this a go and see if it works out' attitude. They recognise where they need to improve, and actively seek out support in order to address those areas.

A former parent governor of our school talked me through her son's primary school experience a couple of years ago. I knew the school had a national reputation for excellence, as did the head teacher, and a string of Outstanding Ofsted reports. She told me bluntly, 'It may well be Outstanding, but it was anything but that for my son. They didn't want to know him at all.'

How many of us can truly say that we do a good job, at the very least, for every single one of our children?

What can be done to ensure children with special needs receive the education they deserve without having to travel long distances to highly specialist provisions?

I stated in Chapter 5 that the 115 children in my school come from an area covering 1,200 square miles, compared to the 1,400 pupils at our local secondary school who come from a catchment area of just six square miles. The distances our pupils, and those in many other special schools, travel each day are vast, as are the costs to the taxpayer associated with that (our host LA has an annual SEN transport bill of approximately £25 million pounds).

I admit above that there will always be young people with cognitive, emotional or therapeutic needs that are so complex and require such expertise that there is no real prospect of receiving a high-quality education in their local school. So, what is to be done instead? And, more importantly, who is to do it, if we are to improve the current state of affairs so that more young people with learning difficulties can receive the high-quality education and support to which they are entitled closer to home?

Everyone has a role to play here. Those roles are interrelated and sometimes, but not always, perfectly aligned. As my former Chair of Governors, Brad Goodwin, is fond of saying, 'We've all got skin in the game.' If the inspection framework is levelled up so that it is no longer more difficult for schools with intakes with lower prior attainment to be judged as Good or better, if the use of blunt progress targets to determine teacher performance-related pay is ceased by head teachers, if head teachers are held to account for illegally excluding children, then we all stand the best possible chance of providing everything that *all* children in our schools are entitled to.

Some suggestions for the Secretary of State for Education

- Recent legislation has required schools to produce SEN Information Reports, which should be available on their websites, that detail their provision for children with SEN. These are designed to help parents in the initial stages of searching for a school for their child. These could be extended: schools could be asked to publish an annual appendix to this report, giving details on the progress the children with SEN in the school are making now. It could provide whole-school and comparative academic progress information, split into sections (whole-school/students with EHCPs/students on SEN support) on the following: attendance; fixed-term exclusions; permanent exclusions; percentage of students in the school with EHCPs compared to local, regional and national figures; percentage of students in the school on SEN support compared to local, regional and national figures.

- There are many schools out there that deserve to have their superb work with children with learning difficulties publicised and lauded. Following the example set by former Minister of State for Schools, David Laws (who wrote to schools that were particularly successful with children entitled to free school meals), these schools need to receive recognition from the DfE. It needs to become a badge of honour to be celebrated – not a worry that a school will develop a reputation and thus become a magnet for more children with SEN.

- Stop prefacing announcements with 'All children must ...'. This creates unnecessary uncertainty among head teachers as we try to figure out which students will, in reality, be included. The evolution of EBacc coverage is a current case in point. It started out as an 'All children will ...' policy and currently there is an expectation from the DfE that 90% of children will do it.

- Without delay, create two new clear routes in to the profession for people wanting to train to be teachers in special schools: one route for those who are new to working in schools and one for teaching assistants (or therapists, for that matter) who wish to remain in their current school but attain qualified teacher status.

- Insist on mandatory co-siting of specialist provision with every mainstream school that is rebuilt on its current site, or when new schools are built. This would mean primary schools with specialist units, and for secondary schools it would mean provision mostly for young people with moderate learning difficulties and/or high-functioning autism. I estimate that 50% of the pupils in my school could be well educated in *any* mainstream school with the right curriculum and support, this would prevent many students with moderate learning needs travelling the excessive distances mentioned previously. The savings on the huge transport costs noted would also be welcome.

- Set aside some money right now, and get your best civil servants planning how you intend to tackle the issues that will arise from your own department's projection of a 31% increase in the number of children requiring a place in a special school from 2015 to 2024 (from the current 87,000 to 114,000).[6] The infrastructure problems and certain increase in costs this could create for local authorities could break them financially.

Some suggestions for Ofsted

- Abolish the grade of Outstanding and the overall judgement (as I argued in Chapter 4).

- Address the problem created by an inspection framework that is loaded against schools with intakes of students with relatively low prior attainment, as one of your staff members is reported to have admitted (see Chapter 4).

- Institute a separate limiting judgement on outcomes for pupils with SEN. Sixth forms and Early Years settings receive separate judgements in the current framework. This judgement should also refer to a school's compliance (or otherwise) with the statutory duties set out by the Equality Act (2010) and its accompanying Regulations.

Some suggestions for senior officers of local authorities

- Tackle illegal exclusion firmly to ensure this becomes a thing of the past.

- You are already aware of the significant variation that exists in your schools regarding the proportions of children with EHCPs or on SEN support. This variation is partly responsible for the millions of pounds that are spent annually on school transport for children with SEN, which is invisible to all but those either working closely with the transport companies or paying for it. My host local authority pays in the region of £25 million pounds a year to transport its children with SEN all over the county and beyond – often past many other perfectly good schools. My children's local primary school has a catchment of a neat one square mile for 240 children. Their local secondary school draws 1,400 students from a six-square-mile footprint. The 115 children in my school live in an area of 1,200 square miles. Making schools provide the education these students are entitled to is a route (a difficult one, I grant you) to saving money, and saving significant travelling times for these students, so that they can attend school much closer to home.

- Ensure your mainstream schools are able to cope with an increase in places for children with EHCPs in the coming decade as per the DfE's projected 31% increase in the special school population as previously noted. There is absolutely no way that the capacity in the special school sector will increase by the same amount in that time (or even get close), so you have two options: (1) send those children with EHCPs who are left when you run out of places to independent special schools (at a massive, unaffordable cost to your schools budget), or (2) send those students with the least challenging SEN (who would have traditionally gone to a special school in your LA) to mainstream schools.

- Ensure your schools (both mainstream and special) are ready for the increase in demand for specialist places for children with autism. This is already happening, and local authorities are struggling to keep pace with it. It will place further stress on an already pressured system in the coming years. Partly due to a change in the way children are being labelled (many children in my school have a primary need of moderate learning difficulties (MLD) but also have autism, but this is changing over time as the labelling of children as having MLD goes out of fashion) and partly to an increase in diagnosis, this is driving an increasing number of young people to be educated in independent special schools, some far from pupils' homes, at considerable cost.

Some suggestions for head teachers

- Be the champion for these children that they, their parents and your colleagues in the SEN department need you to be. Be prepared to tackle any cognitive distortion (ignoring positives, focusing on negatives and predicting failure) that may surface from colleagues.

- Be courageous in your leadership of the curriculum by resisting government diktats and ensuring your curriculum is flexible and responsive enough to prepare all your students for successful adult lives. In some cases this will mean providing high-quality vocational provision, further education (FE) college transition programmes and work placements.

- Be aware of the implications that could be caused by the use of blunt progress targets under your performance-related pay policy. Any that insist on a minimum level of progress for all children are likely to put unnecessary pressure and stress on teachers. Some of the children with SEN they teach may appear – under that measure – to have made poor progress when the opposite may well be true.

- Review your induction programme for new staff. Is there a section on SEN and learning difficulties? I am alarmed by the number of schools in which there is no induction for new teaching assistants beyond standard safeguarding training and a cursory health and safety briefing.

- Consider any unintended messages you may be communicating to prospective parents on tours. You are undoubtedly as proud of the school you serve as I am of ours, but parents' radar may be activated by language that describes your school as academic, that tells parents that you only do GCSEs and, by implication, nothing of a vocational nature or, as is needed for some, Functional Skills or Entry Level qualifications, or that you've never had a child in the school with, say, Williams syndrome before and wouldn't know what to do.

- Take a deeper look at the trends in your use of fixed-term and permanent exclusion, and for sanctions and consequences for your children with SEN. Is there evidence of repeated use, indicating that the particular sanction lacks effectiveness? Have you given full consideration to any of the needs of the child that could be better met in a different way? (I cannot recommend enough the support of speech and language therapists and occupational therapists when considering this.)

- Use the free SEN self-evaluation template developed by the London Leadership Strategy[7] as a way of focusing on areas for improvement, and for reassurance that your areas of strength are recognised and celebrated.

Some suggestions for SENCos

- Use the comprehensive free SEN self-evaluation template developed by the London Leadership Strategy as a self-evaluation tool. This can be used to inform your conversations with other senior leaders and the head teacher about areas that you know the school could improve upon.

- Consider whether the transition arrangements for children joining and leaving your school give sufficient attention to parents and siblings. Getting this right will be a massive early win for your school, and will start off the relationship well.

- Be very clear about the success (or otherwise) of any interventions in place. Some children may be making no more progress than if they were in the class with their peers, but if they are out of class they are losing opportunities to develop social and language skills that they may need. If this is the case, you must question whether the interventions are necessary or appropriate.

- Ask your local special school if all new colleagues can spend some time in their school as part of a comprehensive induction programme with SEN as a key feature. They will be only too happy to oblige.

- While you're there, ask the special school if your colleagues can piggyback onto their professional development programme.

Some suggestions for teachers and teaching assistants

- Seek the advice and support of colleagues in your local special school if you want to feel more confident about assessing the progress your children with SEN are making. It can be difficult to feel you are doing a good job if their progress seems slower than others (it may well be), but they may well be doing spectacularly well. Support in making these judgements can do much for your confidence.

- Are you aware of how much time your children with learning difficulties spend being taught by a teaching assistant? This can easily creep to becoming most or almost all of the day/week, and become 'presenteeism' – the child is in the room, but is effectively in a class of one child. A teaching assistant may be doing a good job, but if a child is rarely, or ever, taught by the teacher, then consideration needs to be given to the effectiveness of that strategy.

- Are you aware of how much time your children with learning difficulties are spending outside of the class, either because of interventions or because their desk is in a corridor? Consider whether the work done in interventions could be done within the classroom, with a little creative differentiation in your planning. Time spent away from peers is time when social skills, language development and a child's feelings of belonging to a tribe are lost.

- Ask the therapist(s) who are working with your children to conduct some of their sessions in your class, so that you and your colleagues can learn how best to support those children with their therapeutic and independence needs. It will also make you a better teacher, as you will realise how you can weave those support strategies into your daily practice.

Notes

1. A. Dyson et al., *Inclusion and Pupil Achievement* (London: Department for Education and Skills, 2004). Research Report RR578. Available at: http://webarchive. nationalarchives.gov.uk/20130401151715/http://www.education.gov.uk/ publications/eOrderingDownload/RR578.pdf.
2. Dyson et al., *Inclusion and Pupil Achievement*, p. 12.
3. See https://www.gov.uk/government/statistics/ special-educational-needs-in-england-january-2015.
4. See http://schoolsweek.co.uk/ the-key-points-from-the-department-for-educations-pupil-projection-figures/.
5. See https://cherrylkd.wordpress.com/2015/01/07/ secure-childrens-homes-a-guest-interview-with-richardalbery84/.
6. See http://schoolsweek.co.uk/ the-key-points-from-the-department-for-educations-pupil-projection-figures/.
7. See http://londonleadershipstrategy.com/content/sen-review-guidance.

Chapter 9

Fear Wants Nothing to Change

'Some of those who are frightened of people with intellectual disabilities may never have met anyone with disabilities. [This is] based on a great fear of change; people do not want to be disturbed in their security or have their values system questioned. They do not want to open their hearts to those who are different.'

Jean Vanier, *Becoming Human*, pp. 116–117

Do you know anyone from Bielefeld?

Have you ever been to Bielefeld?

Do you know anyone who's ever been to Bielefeld?

The Bielefeld Conspiracy was originally a joke made by a young German computer science student in 1994. It is a great example of a meme, and revolves around the idea that the German town of Bielefeld doesn't actually exist. Even the German Chancellor, Angela Merkel, joined in with the fun after attending a meeting in Bielefeld – 'if it exists at all,' she joked. We can prove that Bielefeld doesn't exist because, the satire goes, not one single person can answer yes to any of the three questions above.

It is less funny if you replace 'Bielefeld' with 'special school'.

Do you know anyone from a special school?

Have you ever been to a special school?

Do you know anyone who's ever been to a special school?

Too many of us cannot answer any of these questions in the affirmative. This needs to change, and it needs to change at an institutional as well as a personal level.

The first training session I ever had as a Special Constable with Thames Valley Police was on the murder of Stephen Lawrence, the subsequent Macpherson Report, racism and institutional racism. There is no doubt that the subject was, and remains, a critical one, but it was the first thing we *ever* discussed. We hadn't yet been issued with uniforms, weren't sworn in as warranted officers, and didn't know one end of a baton from the other. At the time my fellow officers and I found this striking. We didn't even know how to caution someone, yet at 9am on Day One we were delving into the details, implications and reverberations of a murder that had happened over ten years previously in another force's area.

This tells you how seriously all police services took the Macpherson Report on the inquiry into Stephen Lawrence's death. Stephen was murdered in London in 1993, and the Macpherson Report labelled the Metropolitan Police as institutionally racist. Much of our training as Special Constables was carried out in good humour and was very enjoyable. This long session was different; it left us in no doubt how seriously the police service viewed the findings of the report.

What will it take for the services, establishments or authorities that exist to work with children with learning difficulties and disabilities or other forms of SEN to be labelled 'institutionally disablist'? You would hope that it wouldn't take an event as extreme as the death of a child or young person and the uncovering of failings of professionals trained and paid to keep them safe.

Too late – that's already happened.

On 19 March 2013, 18-year-old Connor Sparrowhawk, who had autism and epilepsy, was admitted to Slade House, an NHS assessment and treatment unit in Oxfordshire.

On 4 July 2013, he was found unconscious in a bath at Slade House, and subsequently died. A post-mortem showed that he had drowned, probably as a result of an epileptic seizure. Southern Health NHS Foundation Trust attributed his death to natural causes, but an independent investigation demanded by Connor's family concluded his death could have been prevented.[1] The report states that Connor's epilepsy was not properly assessed or managed, which led to poor decisions being made around his care. It further found there was unsafe supervision at bath times, no family involvement in his assessment and care, and no effective clinical leadership.

The jury at the inquest at Oxford Coroner's Court, which concluded in October 2015, found that 'neglect contributed to Connor's death'. They also concluded that there were serious failings by the trust, noting that there had been 'inadequate communication with Connor's family, as well as inadequate training and supervision'.[2]

Connor's tragic death is not an isolated case. Nico Reed, who had athetoid cerebral palsy, was found dead at a supported living home in Oxfordshire in August 2012. The BBC reported the death under the headline 'Disabled man could have been saved':[3] the inquest at Oxfordshire's Coroner's Court heard of concerning staffing levels, that the frequency of checks on residents was below guidelines and that there was an absence of a risk assessment for Nico.

Two cases, tragic as they clearly were, could be argued by some as being regrettable but isolated incidents. The standard 'lessons will be learned' spiel will come spilling out of someone's mouth after an inquest, with assurances that this kind of thing will never happen again.

But they are not isolated.

Southern Health NHS Trust, the organisation that was supposed to keep Connor Sparrowhawk safe, has been found to have 'failed to investigate the unexpected deaths of more than 1,000 people since 2011', many of whom had learning difficulties.[4] Mazars, the firm carrying out the investigation, found that only 4% of unexpected deaths of patients with a learning difficulty were investigated as a critical or serious incident.[5]

4%.

This pitiful number is only compounded by the statistic revealing that those individuals with a learning difficulty, on average, die aged 56[6] – a full seven years younger than the average age at death of Learning Disability service users (what a clinical phrase) over 18 across all NHS Trusts included in the Confidential Inquiry into Premature Deaths of People with Learning Disabilities (CIPOLD).[7] This is indicative of the value that society places on the lives of people with learning difficulties. One could argue that this organisation that was set up to care and support people with learning difficulties decided that the circumstances surrounding the deaths of hundreds of people weren't worth investigating. The leadership team remains in place following the publication of the CQC report in April 2016 which was critical of the quality of leadership.[8] Only the Chairman, Mike Petter left his post, having resigned in April 2016 after significant and sustained criticism.

Contrast this with the pressure that was brought to bear by the media on the Chairman of the Environment Agency, Sir Philip Dilley, following the severe flooding in Yorkshire and Lancashire in the Christmas period of 2015. Sir Philip was on holiday in Barbados at the time of the flooding and was heavily criticised for not appearing in public when Storm Eva battered parts of the UK.

The Chief Executive, Sir James Bevan, the operational head of the agency, was in command at the time, yet the Chairman had to step down because of public expectation that he be in the UK and show his face in the event of a severe flooding event. Being in the wrong part of the world and not returning quickly enough was a resigning matter in this case, as it indicated a lack of appreciation of the seriousness of the situation. It had nothing to do with his command of the situation. Sir Philip was the Chairman. Not Chief Executive. Chairman. And yet in the case of Southern Health, the leadership team still remain in post. Following such critical reports from Mazars and the CQC one wonders what they would have to do to get the sack. If there were lessons to be learned, the Trust seemed unable to find out what they were. It's hard not to feel that these people, their lives and their deaths were considered worthless.

In the words of Jean Vanier:

> Fear wants nothing to change; fear demands the status quo.
> And the status quo leads to death. (*Becoming Human*, p. 73)

For those of us who have committed our working lives to these children and their families, and to the children and the families themselves, it feels like we are in our own deadly serious version of the Bielefeld Conspiracy.

Yet these children, their families, their physical, emotional and intellectual needs, their immense daily challenges and the schools they go to do exist, regardless of the fear that some may have of them. They are invisible to many because a choice has been made not to see them. It is the wrong choice.

How many more years will go by before children with learning difficulties can say the following?

I am no longer more likely to die earlier than you.

I am no longer more likely to be bullied than you.

I am no longer more likely to receive a fixed-term exclusion from school than you.

I am no longer more likely to receive a permanent exclusion from school than you.

I am no longer less likely to work than you.

I am no longer more likely to be paid less than you.

I am no longer more likely to live in poverty than you.

I am no longer more likely to have mental health problems as a child than you.

I am no longer more likely to have children with their own learning difficulties than you.

I am no longer more likely to end up in prison than you.

We all have to want the life chances and opportunities of children and young people with learning difficulties to be better – to get closer to those you and I enjoy, to those our children enjoy. We all have to want to confront the fear that sits within us, as Jean Vanier describes so powerfully above. We all have to choose to commit to recognising that society, as it is today, is a difficult place for these young people to thrive; to acknowledge that this is not right; that such a state of affairs must change; and that we all have a part to play in making that change happen.

And the first step is to see these children.

Notes

1. *Bindmans*, 'Death of 18-year-old Connor Sparrowhawk was preventable' (24 February 2014). Available at: http://www.bindmans.com/news-and-events/news-article/death-of-18-year-old-connor-sparrowhawk-was-preventable.
2. *BBC News*, 'Connor Sparrowhawk inquest: Care unit death "contributed to by neglect"' (16 October 2015). Available at: http://www.bbc.co.uk/news/uk-england-oxfordshire-34548638.
3. *BBC News*, 'Disabled man "could have been saved"' (12 December 2014). Available at: http://www.bbc.co.uk/news/uk-england-oxfordshire-30441266.
4. See M. Buchanan, 'NHS trust "failed to investigate hundreds of deaths"', *BBC News* (10 December 2015). Available at: http://www.bbc.co.uk/news/health-35051845.
5. Mazars, *Independent review of deaths of people with a Learning Disability or Mental Health problem in contact with Southern Health NHS Foundation Trust April 2011 to March 2015*: (2015). Available at: https://www.england.nhs.uk/south/wp-content/uploads/sites/6/2015/12/mazars-rep.pdf, p. 15.
6. Mazars, *Independent review of deaths*, p. 16.
7. Mazars, *Independent review of deaths*, p. 29.
8. See Care Quality Commission, *Southern Health NHS Foundation Trust Quality Report* (2016). Available at: http://www.cqc.org.uk/sites/default/files/new_reports/AAAF4191.pdf.

Postscript

On 17 March 2016 England's Department for Education published its latest White Paper, *Educational excellence everywhere*.[1] In her foreword, Nicky Morgan stated that, 'this white paper sets out our plans for the next five years, building on and extending our reforms to achieve educational excellence everywhere.' Everywhere is the most important word in that sentence. If the department truly mean everywhere, then it surely follows that they also mean everyone (as we saw in Chapter 6)?

The main thrust of the White Paper is the ideological belief, flying in the face of all the evidence, that standards will rise if all schools become academies by 2022. Academies are state schools that receive their funding directly from central government and are free of local authority control, as opposed to maintained schools which remain part of a local authority. (It is worth noting at this point that the school I lead is an academy.)

The intense opposition that this proposal provoked resulted in the then Secretary of State for Education, Nicky Morgan, backing down barely seven weeks later, announcing that schools that were already performing well should retain the choice on whether to become an academy. Given that schools continue to convert, and that Nicky Morgan retained the right to convert schools where local authorities are deemed to be underperforming or become financially unviable, it is clear that all she has done is remove the 2022 deadline. We are a way down the road to total academisation, whether we like it or not.

I am deeply concerned that a system where all state schools are academies further disadvantages children with learning difficulties. The policy is predicated on the false notion that academies, specifically multi-academy trusts (MATs) which are groups of academies formally and legally bound together, are leaner, more ambitious and more innovative than local authorities. Here's the rub. Local authorities take responsibility for *all* children who live in their patch. They have a geographical commitment to providing for all children. MATs have no such commitment to any given local area – even those MATs that consist entirely of local, proximal schools will still have only a partial commitment as there are some students they won't have to consider: either because of age or gender, but more likely because of special educational needs. Once all schools become academies, local authorities will simply become commissioners of services and school places as they'll still retain the responsibility for ensuring all of their children are in school somewhere. They'll then need to commission places where there are gaps. This is likely to leave local authorities having to seek places elsewhere, such as at special schools like mine or in expensive independent special schools.

I foresee this being exacerbated by the inevitable diminution of local authority SEN support services. Local authorities currently offer a range of support services, including but not limited to SEN services. These are typically, but not always, free at the point of need and inevitably are of varying quality. At the very least, though, they exist. As local authorities shrink, these services will cease to exist, or exist on a traded service basis and compete with the market, the solution so beloved of right-wing politicians.

This is how I see that playing out at the chalkface:

> A teacher, looking exhausted and exasperated and on the verge of tears, enters the office of the SENCo clutching a sheaf of papers and sits down.
>
> 'I need some help,' she says. 'We're trying everything, but Kieran's progress is agonisingly slow and we're all out of ideas. The class team feel like we're failing him and the parents are starting to get really concerned.'
>
> 'OK, let me give the learning and language support service a call. They've really helped us in the past,' replies the SENCo.
>
> The number you have dialled has not been recognised…
>
> 'That's weird. I'll try the behaviour support team. They're great…'
>
> The number you have dialled has not been recognised…
>
> 'Uh, what about the autism support team? They're always generous with their time and will offer some really helpful strategies…'
>
> The number you have dialled has not been recognised…
>
> 'Let me make one more call. Hi, yes is that the borough special needs manager? Great. Look, I'm trying to get hold of your support teams and none of the numbers seem to be working. What? What do you mean

they don't exist any more? Where do I get our support from? We BUY it? From where?'[2]

The trading arms of MATs or businesses will run the back-office functions that were previously the preserve of the LA, such as human resources, payroll, IT technical support and financial services. These are easy to set up, easy to staff and are universally needed – show me a school that has no need for IT support these days. But there is little or no incentive for MATs or businesses to have their own specialist physical and sensory support teams, autism specialists and the like. Indeed, this could be deemed to be risky as they then become the local centre of excellence for, say, autism and consequently become attractive to prospective parents.

My biggest fear is that conversations like the one above end with the head teacher calling the local authority to request an emergency review for Kieran so they can organise a change of placement as they state that they can't meet his needs any longer.

Where does he go? The choices will be slim. There is precedent here that we first encountered in Chapter 4 – as the Office of the Children's Commissioner found, too often these children are told, 'It might be best if you looked elsewhere.'

But when all schools are academies and support for children with learning difficulties is reduced to almost nothing, the danger is there may be no mainstream places left to look.

Notes

1. Department for Education, *Educational Excellence Everywhere* (March 2016). Available at: https://www.gov.uk/government/publications/educational-excellence-everywhere.
2. This excerpt originally appeared in J. O'Brien, 'White Paper: How SEND is the Achilles' heel of mass academisation', *TES* [blog] (27 March 2016). Available at: https://www.tes.com/news/school-news/breaking-views/white-paper-how-send-achilles-heel-mass-academisation.

Glossary

Academy: State-funded schools in England which are directly funded by the Department for Education and independent of local authority control. The terms of the arrangements are set out in individual academy Funding Agreements. Academies do not have to stick to the national curriculum or to adhere to national standards for teacher pay and conditions.

Annual review: The review of an EHCP carried out by schools every 12 months as a minimum. All the professionals involved in the education of the child are invited to attend along with the parents.

Asperger syndrome: A form of autism (see below). While Asperger syndrome has similarities to autism, people with Asperger syndrome have fewer problems with speaking and are often of average, or above average, intelligence. It is differentiated from high-functioning autism (see below) in that people with Asperger syndrome will typically not have had delayed language development when younger. Asperger syndrome is not usually accompanied by the learning difficulties that can be associated with autism, but may be accompanied by specific learning difficulties, such as dyslexia and dyspraxia, or other conditions such as attention deficit hyperactivity disorder (ADHD) and epilepsy.

Attention deficit hyperactivity disorder (ADHD): A set of behavioural symptoms that include hyperactivity, impulsiveness and inattentiveness. Common symptoms include: restlessness; a short attention span or being easily distracted; overactivity or constant fidgeting; and impulsivity. Can occur in people of any intellectual ability, although it is more common in people with learning difficulties. People with ADHD may also have additional problems, such as sleep and anxiety disorders.

Autism: The National Autistic Society defines autism as, 'A lifelong, developmental disability that affects how a person communicates with and relates to other people, and how they experience the world around them.'[1] The characteristics of autism vary from person to person, but are generally divided into three main groups (the so-called 'triad of impairments'): difficulty with social communication; difficulty with social interaction; difficulty with social imagination. People with autism may have: a love of routines; sensory sensitivity; special interests; or learning disabilities. The terms 'ASD' and 'autism' tend to be used interchangeably.

Autistic spectrum disorder (ASD): See **Autism.**

Behavioural, emotional and social difficulties (BESD): See **Emotional and behavioural difficulties (EBD).**

Cerebral palsy: The general term for a number of neurological conditions that affect movement and coordination. Cerebral palsy is caused by a problem in the parts of the brain responsible for controlling muscles and can occur due to damage to the brain before, during or shortly after birth or if there are abnormalities in the development of the brain. Cerebral palsy can be caused by premature birth, difficulties during pregnancy, gene mutations that affect brain development, bleeding in the baby's brain or by an infection caught by the mother during pregnancy.

Child and Adolescent Mental Health Services (CAMHS): Services designed to assess and treat children and young people with emotional, behavioural or mental health difficulties. CAMHS provide a wide range of services from basic pastoral care, such as identifying mental health problems, to highly specialist services, known as 'Tier 4', which provide in-patient care for those with a severe mental illness.

Children and young people's secure estate: This comprises three types of establishment – secure children's homes (SCH), secure training centres (STC) and young offender institutions (YOI). Young people who are offenders under the age of 18 (or in some cases aged 18 but remaining in the under-18 estate) will be held in either a secure children's home, a secure training centre or a young offender institution. The Youth Justice Board is responsible for placing young people in custody. Typically, those aged under 15 will be held in an SCH and those over 15 will be held in either an STC or YOI. (Note that since 2013 YOIs no longer hold girls.) YOIs holding young people operate within many of the same rules and policies as prisons for men and women.

Children's Commissioner: A number of children's sector charities called for the creation of the post of Children's Commissioner. The Victoria Climbié Inquiry, chaired by Lord Laming, recommended that a National Agency for Children and Families should be created whose chief executive would have the functions of a Children's Commissioner for England. The main functions of the agency include assessing and advising on the impact on children and families of any proposed changes in policy and, powerfully, at its discretion, conducting serious case reviews or overseeing those carried out by other agencies. The post of Children's Commissioner was established by the Children Act 2004 and its remit strengthened by the Children and Families Act 2014. The Children's Commissioner has a statutory duty to promote and protect the rights of all children in England, in accordance with the United Nations Convention on the Rights of the Child. The Children and Families Act 2014 gives the Children's Commissioner special responsibility for the rights of children who are in or leaving care, living away from home or receiving social care services.

Down syndrome: A genetic condition caused by the presence of an extra chromosome 21 in the body's cells. It is not a disease. In the majority of cases, Down syndrome is not an inherited condition. Down syndrome usually occurs because of a chance happening at the time of conception. All children with Down syndrome have some degree of learning disability and delayed development, but this varies widely between individuals. Around 1 in every 10 children with Down syndrome also experiences additional difficulties such as ASD or ADHD. Some children with Down syndrome have very few health problems as a result of their condition. Others will experience several of the more common health conditions associated with Down syndrome, and will need extra medical care and attention. These include:

- Heart problems – around half of children with Down syndrome are born with a congenital heart defect.

- Gut problems – many people with Down syndrome have some sort of problem with their digestive system. Constipation, diarrhoea and indigestion are all common, as are more serious problems such as small bowel obstruction, which stops food passing from the stomach into the large bowel. Some children also develop coeliac disease (a condition in which someone has an adverse reaction to gluten) and reflux.

- Hearing problems – most people with Down syndrome have problems with their hearing. This is often temporary, but it can sometimes be permanent.

- Vision problems – many people with Down syndrome also have problems with their eyesight and often need to wear glasses.

- Thyroid problems – around 1 in 10 people with Down syndrome has problems with their thyroid gland, mostly hypothyroidism, which means their thyroid gland is underactive.

- Increased risk of infections – people with Down syndrome are more likely to develop infections, such as pneumonia, because their immune system has not developed properly.

- Dementia – there is a tendency for people with Down syndrome to develop dementia at a younger age than in the general population, usually from about 40 years of age onwards (although it's not inevitable that everyone with Down syndrome will develop dementia).

Education, Health and Care Plan (EHCP): An EHCP details the education, health and social care support that is to be provided to a child or young person who has SEN or a disability. It is drawn up by the local authority after an EHCP needs assessment of the child or young person has determined that an EHCP is necessary, and after consultation with relevant partner agencies. It is a legally enforceable document designed to ensure that the child receives all the support to which they are entitled. It has replaced the statement of SEN (see **Statement**). In 2014, 2.8% of children of school age had a statement or EHCP, a figure that has remained at this level since 2007.[2]

Emotional and behavioural difficulties (EBD): A recently outdated term, but one that is still in common usage, to describe a subset of SEN which manifest themselves primarily as difficulty regulating emotions and behaviours. Also called SEBD or BESD, with the 'S' referring to social difficulties. Superseded by social, emotional and mental health difficulties (SEMH) (see below) in the new SEN Code of Practice.

158

English Baccalaureate (EBacc): A performance measure for schools in England, first applied in the 2010 school performance tables. It measures the achievement of pupils who have gained Key Stage 4 (GCSE level) qualifications in the following subjects: English, maths, history or geography, the sciences, and a language.

Eye-gaze technology: This enables a person to use eye movements to operate a computer or tablet. Eye-gaze technology is typically used by children and adults who have a significant physical disability, who have no speech, or whose speech is difficult to understand.

Fixed-term exclusion (FTE): When a child is barred from attending school for a defined period of time. Fixed-term exclusions can only amount to a maximum of 45 school days per child in any one school year. If a child is sent home during the course of a day then this is regarded as half a day of fixed-term exclusion. Only head teachers have the power to exclude children. Head teachers must write to parents after each period of fixed-term exclusion, explaining the reasons for exclusion, informing parents of their right to appeal the decision, and letting them know how they can do that. A challenge to a fixed-term exclusion can be made if a child has been excluded for more than five school days in a term or an exclusion will mean they will miss a public exam or national curriculum test. For exclusions of five school days or less, parents can ask the governing body to consider their views. If a child has been excluded for a fixed period, schools should set and mark work for the first five school days. If the exclusion is longer than five school days, the school must arrange full-time education from the sixth school day.

Foetal alcohol syndrome disorder (FASD): A result of alcohol consumption by the mother during pregnancy. FASD is an umbrella term that covers foetal alcohol syndrome (FAS), alcohol-related neurodevelopmental disorder, alcohol-related birth defects, foetal alcohol effects and partial foetal alcohol syndrome (pFAS). Its effects range from learning difficulties and ADHD to heart problems. FASD may not be detected at birth but can become apparent later in life, and carries lifelong implications. The prevalence of FASD in the UK and internationally is not accurately known. Some characteristics of FASD include: attention and memory deficits; hyperactivity; difficulty with abstract concepts; poor problem-solving skills; difficulty learning from consequences; social, emotional and behavioural difficulties and poor impulse control.

Children with FASD can present with some physical effects (but these are not always observed) such as smaller head circumference; heart problems; damage to limbs, kidneys, the structure of the brain or eyes; hearing issues; specific facial characteristics, including a flat nasal bridge, upturned nose, thin upper lip and smooth philtrum (the vertical groove between the upper lip and nose).

Fragile X syndrome: A genetic condition that is the most common known cause of inherited learning disabilities. In the UK it is found in around 1 in 4,000 males and 1 in 6,000 females. There are a wide range of characteristics associated with fragile X, but they are not all present in every case. Learning disabilities occur in almost all males with fragile X to differing degrees, but severe learning disabilities is rare. Girls usually have milder learning disabilities than boys and may have concentration problems and social, emotional and communication difficulties related to extreme shyness and anxiety in social situations, but some girls with fragile X may be clinically unaffected. As well as learning disabilities, common behavioural characteristics include short attention span, distractibility, impulsiveness, restlessness, overactivity and sensory problems. Many children and adults show autistic-like traits and some may receive a dual diagnosis of autism. Speech and language skills are usually delayed, with continuing speech and communication problems. Some children and adults develop epilepsy. However, strengths associated with fragile X include visual learning ability and long-term memory. People with fragile X are also often described as being sensitive to others' emotions and having a good sense of humour. There are some physical features associated with fragile X, including a long, narrow face with prominent jaw bones and ears, but these characteristics may be less prominent in young children. The lack of distinguishing features is one of the reasons that diagnosis can be delayed. The only way to tell if someone has fragile X syndrome is via a genetic test.

Free school meals (FSM): Available to any child, from those at nursery full-time up to sixth-form students and those aged 16–18 in further education. Children are eligible if parents are in receipt of Universal Credit; Income Support; Income-based Jobseeker's Allowance; Income-related Employment and Support Allowance; Support under Part VI of the Immigration and Asylum Act 1999; the Guarantee element of State Pension Credit; and Child Tax Credit, provided they are not entitled to

Working Tax Credit and have an annual income of £16,190 or less, as assessed by Her Majesty's Revenue and Customs. Children who receive a qualifying benefit in their own right are also eligible to receive free school meals.

Further education (FE) college: A college providing education to young people over the compulsory school age of 16. The FE sector in England includes general further education colleges, sixth-form colleges, specialist colleges for young people with SEN and those catering solely for adults.

High-functioning autism: A term applied to people with autism who are of average or above average intelligence. Differentiated from **Asperger syndrome** in that people with Asperger syndrome will typically not have had delayed language development when younger.

Hypertonia: A condition in which someone has excessive muscle tone so that arms or legs, for example, are stiff and therefore difficult to move. Hypertonia occurs when the areas of the brain or spinal cord that control muscle contraction are damaged. Medication to relax the muscles can be used to ease hypertonia, with Botulinum toxin (Botox) often used to target a specific area of the body because its effects are local, but the effects wear off after a time, so Botox injections have to be repeated on a regular basis.

Independent Review Panel (IRP): Parents have the right to request that the decision to exclude their child be reviewed. If they exercise this right an Independent Review Panel, with authority from sections 7, 16 and 25 of the School Discipline (Pupil Exclusion and Reviews) (England) Regulation 2012, is convened to review the decision of a governing body if that body has upheld a school's decision to exclude a pupil.

Their remit is to ensure that a decision to uphold an exclusion is impartial and independent. IRPs consist of either three or five members appointed by the local authority with a lay member, head teacher, governor of a maintained school, member of a pupil referral unit or director of an academy on the panel. To avoid an obvious conflict of interest none of the panel may be directly involved with the relevant excluding school. A local authority-appointed clerk advises the parties on matters of law and procedure. IRPs cannot reinstate a permanently excluded pupil.

Looked-after child (LAC) (also known as a 'child in care'): A child who is being looked after by the local authority (who have legal responsibility for that child). They might be living with foster parents, at home with their parents under the supervision of social services, or in a residential setting such as a children's home, residential school or secure unit. Children can be placed in care voluntarily by parents struggling to cope, or children's services may have intervened because the child was at significant risk of harm.

Maintained schools: Schools that are overseen, or 'maintained', by local authorities. They must follow the national curriculum and national standards for teacher pay and conditions.

Moderate learning difficulties (MLD): Pupils with moderate learning difficulties will generally be working at a level well below that expected of children their age. This is likely to extend across most or all areas of the curriculum. It is highly likely that they will have much greater difficulty than their peers in acquiring basic literacy and numeracy skills, problems with working memory and in acquiring knowledge and understanding concepts. They may also have difficulties associated with a speech and language delay, social, emotional and behavioural difficulties or physical difficulties associated with certain conditions. MLD commonly accompanies, or is strongly linked to, conditions such as Down syndrome, Williams syndrome or fragile X syndrome.

National curriculum: A mandatory curriculum for maintained schools, but not for academies and free schools. It determines what should be taught and sets attainment targets for learning, determining also how performance will be assessed and reported.

National Professional Qualification for Headship (NPQH): A course run by the National College of Teaching and Leadership for teachers in preparation for becoming head teachers. Previously, this was mandatory for all new head teachers, but this requirement has now been relaxed.

Occupational therapy (OT): A health care profession that provides practical support to enable people to facilitate recovery and overcome any barriers that prevent them from doing the activities that matter to them. It aims to increase people's independence and satisfaction in all aspects of life. 'Occupation' refers to the activities that allow people to live independently. This could be essential day-to-day tasks such as self-care, work or leisure.

Ofsted: Office for Standards in Education, a non-Ministerial government department set up under the Education (Schools) Act 1992 to take responsibility for all school inspections in England. Her Majesty's Inspectors (HMI) are its professional arm.

Parent Partnership Service: This had a duty to provide information, advice and support to disabled children and young people, and those with SEN, and their parents. Now known as the Information, Advice and Support (IAS) Service. There should be an IAS Service in every local authority.

Pathological demand avoidance syndrome (PDA): Considered to be part of the autism spectrum (see **Autism**). The main difficulty for people with PDA is that an anxiety-based need to be in control drives the avoidance of demands and expectations. The areas of social understanding and communication skills are strengths of those with PDA in comparison to others on the spectrum. PDA can be characterised by: avoidance of the ordinary demands of life; appearing sociable, but with a superficial depth in understanding; excessive mood swings and impulsivity; language delay; and obsessive behaviour, often focused on people.

Permanent exclusion (PX): When a child is permanently barred from attending a school, following a serious breach, or persistent breaches, of the school's behaviour policy; and where allowing the child to remain in school would seriously harm the education or welfare of the child or others in the school.

Personal Education Plan (PEP): An element of a care plan maintained by a local authority, which sets out the educational needs of a looked-after child. Reviewed every six months and, if a looked-after child also has an EHCP, one of the two PEP reviews should, where possible, coincide with the EHCP annual review.

Pica: Eating or mouthing non-edible items. Reasons for experiencing pica could be medical, dietary, sensory or behavioural, and could include: not understanding that some things are inedible; sensory-seeking behaviour satisfied by the texture or the taste of an item; relieving anxiety, stress, pain or discomfort; a continuing of infant mouthing behaviour, or a later occurrence of the mouthing phase.

Prader–Willi syndrome (PWS): A complex medical condition which requires the person with PWS to need extra support with their health and development and in both education and work. People with PWS may present with some challenging learning and emotional behaviours and a range of medical issues such as low muscle tone with associated motor development delays, short stature if not treated with growth hormone, and incomplete sexual development. Initial difficulties in feeding after birth are common, but early childhood sees an increased appetite, which can lead to excessive eating and obesity which can be life-threatening. There are characteristic facial and other physical features of PWS, including: almond-shaped eyes; a narrow forehead; a down-turned mouth with a triangular-shaped upper lip; and small hands and feet. Poor large muscle strength and tone with associated difficulties in coordination and balance can be improved with therapy and exercise. Small muscle strength is usually better. Most people with PWS have borderline or moderate learning difficulties, while a minority have severe learning difficulties.

Prevent: From 1 July 2015 all schools and childcare providers have had the duty (under section 26 of the Counter-Terrorism and Security Act 2015) to have 'due regard to the need to prevent people from being drawn into terrorism'. This is known as the Prevent duty. It aims to ensure staff are able to identify children who may be vulnerable to radicalisation, and know what to do when they are identified.

Profound and multiple learning difficulties (PMLD): Children and adults with PMLD have more than one disability, the most significant of which is a profound learning disability. All people who have PMLD have great difficulty communicating. In addition, many have sensory or physical disabilities, complex health needs or mental health difficulties which may also affect behaviour. All children and adults with PMLD need high levels of support with most aspects of daily life and are likely to be at least partly dependent on others for support to manage basic self-care tasks such as feeding and toileting.

Progress 8: A performance measure based on students' KS4 progress measured across eight subjects: English, maths, three other EBacc subjects (see **English Baccalaureate**), and three further subjects, which can be from the range of EBacc subjects, or can be any other approved, high-value arts, academic or vocational qualification.

P scales: Attainment targets and performance descriptors for pupils aged 5–16 with SEN who cannot access the national curriculum. They range from P1i to P8. The performance descriptors for P1–P3 are the same across English, maths and science.

Psychotherapy: A therapy that helps people with emotional, social or mental health problems. Psychotherapy usually involves talking, but sometimes other methods may be used – for example, art, music, drama and movement.

Pupil Premium: Funding allocated specifically to schools for each child registered as eligible for free school meals at any point in the past six years. It is £1,320 per year for each child in Reception to Year 6 and £935 for each child in Year 7 to Year 11. Schools must annually publish details of how they spend their Pupil Premium, and the effect this has had on the attainment of the pupils for whom the funding was provided.

Pupil referral unit (PRU): A school established and maintained by a local authority under section 19(2) of the Education Act 1996 that is specially organised to provide education for pupils who would otherwise not receive suitable education because of illness (colloquially known as a medical PRU), or because they are at risk of exclusion or any other reason. Academy versions tend to be called AP Academies (with the AP standing for alternative provision).

Reactive attachment disorder: A condition in which an infant or young child doesn't establish healthy attachments with parents or caregivers. Reactive attachment disorder may develop if the child's basic needs for comfort, affection and nurturing aren't met and loving, caring, stable attachments with others are not established.

Reporting and Analysis for Improvement through school Self-Evaluation (RAISEonline): A web-based DfE/Ofsted tool that provides an interactive analysis of school and student performance data.

School Direct: An initial teacher training programme run by a school or group of schools in partnership with a university or school-centred initial teacher training (SCITT) provider.

Secure children's home (SCH): There are 15 secure children's homes in England and Wales[3] and they range in size from five to 38 beds. They generally accommodate remanded or sentenced young people aged 12–14 and girls and 'at risk' boys up to the age of 16. They have a lower staff to child ratio than either secure training centres or young offender institutions, operating with between one member of staff to two children and six staff to eight children, allowing them to focus on the emotional, physical and mental health needs of the young people they accommodate. The children receive between 25 to 30 hours of education a week, delivered by qualified teachers. As of March 2016 there were 101 children in SCHs.[4]

Secure training centre (STC): There are three STCs in England, which are all run by the private company G4S. STCs hold boys and girls between the ages of 12 and 17 who have been convicted of an offence or are on remand. The staff to child ratio in STCs is higher than in secure children's homes, ranging between two staff to six children and three staff to eight children. As of March 2016 there were 162 children in STCs.[5]

SEN Code of Practice: Government legislation that provides statutory guidance on duties, policies and procedures in relation to children and young people with special educational needs, and disabled children and young people up to the age of 25.

Sensory diet: An occupational therapy intervention strategy devised to attain and maintain appropriate states of attention and arousal throughout each day. A sensory diet consists of a carefully planned programme of specific sensory–motor activities that is scheduled according to each child's needs.

SEN support: The categorisation of a child by a school that recognises the child requires provision to be made for him or her due to an identified special educational need, but the severity does not meet the threshold for the child to have an EHCP. In 2015, 15.4% of all school-aged children in England were identified as having some form of SEN (including those in need of a statement, as it was known then).[6] Interestingly, this figure stood at 21.1% in 2010, leading to debate that schools had previously been categorising students as having SEN unnecessarily when SEN was a factor in measuring a school's performance in so-called contextual value-added terms.

Severe learning difficulties (SLD): Someone with SLD is likely to have a significant impairment in basic awareness and understanding of themselves, of the people around them and of the world they live in. People with SLD will have additional disabilities such as autism, they may display challenging behaviour, other medical issues such as epilepsy and have a severe impairment in their ability to communicate effectively. IQ is sometimes used as an indicator of general learning ability and someone with SLD is described as having an IQ in the range 20 to 35. People with SLD may be at least partly dependent on others for support to manage basic self-care tasks such as feeding and toileting.

Social, emotional and behavioural difficulties (SEBD): See **Emotional and behavioural difficulties**.

Social, emotional and mental health difficulties (SEMH): The new term to replace EBD, SEBD or BESD. The change has been designed to encourage professionals to consider the needs underlying any behavioural difficulties. It is defined in section 6.32 of the 2015 SEN Code of Practice as:

> Children and young people may experience a wide range of social and emotional difficulties which manifest themselves in many ways. These may include becoming withdrawn or isolated, as well as displaying challenging, disruptive or disturbing behaviour. These behaviours may reflect underlying mental health difficulties such as anxiety or depression, self-harming, substance misuse, eating disorders, or physical symptoms that are medically unexplained. Other children and young people may have disorders such as attention deficit disorder, attention deficit hyperactivity disorder or attachment disorder.

Special educational needs (SEN): Used interchangeably with SEND (with the 'D' standing for Disabilities). A child or young person has SEN if they have a learning difficulty or disability which calls for special educational provision to be made for him or her. A child of compulsory school age or a young person has a learning difficulty or disability if he or she has a significantly greater difficulty in learning than the majority of others of the same age, or has a disability which prevents or hinders him or her from making use of facilities of a kind generally provided for others of the same age in mainstream schools or mainstream post-16 institutions.[7]

Special Educational Needs Coordinator (SENCo): A qualified teacher in a school or maintained nursery school with the responsibility for coordinating SEN provision. SENDCo is now also in common usage to mean the same thing.

Special school: A school which is specifically organised to make special educational provision for pupils with SEN. Usually the possession of an EHCP is a condition of entry to such schools.

Specific Learning Difficulties (SpLDs): Difficulties that affect the way information is learned and processed. The difficulties are neurological (rather than psychological), and are not related to the intelligence of the person. They can have a significant impact on education and learning and on the acquisition of literacy skills. SpLD is used to cover a range of difficulties that can co-occur, such as dyslexia, dyspraxia, dyscalculia and ADHD.

Speech and language therapy (SALT): Speech and language therapy is a health care profession there to enable children, young people and adults with speech, language and communication difficulties (and associated difficulties with eating and swallowing known as dysphagia) to reach their maximum communication potential and achieve independence in all aspects of life.

Speech, language and communication needs (SLCN): A range of needs manifesting itself in: speech that may be difficult for the listener(s) to understand; struggling to produce certain sounds, say words or sentences; not understanding words that are being used; not understanding instructions; difficulties in talking to and listening to others.

Statement: A statement of special educational needs was the precursor to the EHCP.

Tracheotomy: An opening created at the front of the neck so a tube can be inserted into the windpipe (trachea) to help a person breathe.

Tribunal (formally the First-tier Tribunal (Special Educational Needs and Disability)): An independent body which has jurisdiction under section 333 of the Education Act 1996 for determining appeals by parents against local authority decisions on whether to carry out EHC needs assessments, whether to grant EHCPs, or on the contents of EHCPs, typically on matters such as the school the child is to attend or on the level of therapy provision for the child. The Tribunal's decision is binding on both parties to the appeal. The Tribunal also hears claims of disability discrimination under the Equality Act 2010.

Vagus nerve stimulation (VNS): The vagus nerves are a pair of nerves that start in the brain and run through the body. VNS aims to treat epilepsy by use of a stimulator (or pulse generator) which is connected, inside the body, to the left vagus nerve in the neck. The stimulator sends regular, mild electrical stimulations to this nerve, with the aim of reducing the number, length and severity of epileptic seizures. The vagus nerve sends these regular stimulations to the brain. The aim is to help calm down the irregular electrical brain activity that leads to seizures. This form of treatment is considered for people whose seizures are not controlled with medication.

White Paper: Policy documents produced by the British government that set out proposals for future legislation. They are the starting point for further consultation and discussion with interested or affected groups and provide space for amendments before a bill is formally presented to parliament.

Williams syndrome: A genetic condition that is present at birth. It is characterised by medical problems, including cardiovascular disease, developmental delays and learning disabilities. Williams syndrome affects 1 in 10,000 people worldwide and is known to occur equally in males and females.

Young offender institution (YOI): There are seven YOIs in England and Wales that hold boys aged 15–18, with six managed by the prison service and one run by a private firm. Four of the seven YOIs only hold boys aged 15–18, while in the remaining three children share a site with adult prisoners. Since 2013 the Youth Justice Board has not placed girls in YOIs. As of March 2016 there were 619 under-18s in YOIs.[8] Staffing in YOIs has the lowest staff to child ratio in the children's secure estate.

Notes

1. See http://www.autism.org.uk/about/what-is.aspx.
2. Department for Education, *Statistical First Release, Special educational needs in England: January 2015* (2015). Available at: https://www.gov.uk/government/uploads/ system/uploads/attachment_data/file/447917/SFR25-2015_Text.pdf, p. 1.
3. See http://www.securechildrenshomes.org.uk/services/.
4. Ministry of Justice and Youth Justice Board for England and Wales, *Youth custody report: March 2016*. Available at: https://www.gov.uk/government/statistics/ youth-custody-data.
5. Ministry of Justice and Youth Justice Board for England and Wales, *Youth custody report: March 2016*. Available at: https://www.gov.uk/government/statistics/ youth-custody-data.
6. Department for Education, *Special educational needs in England: January 2015* (2015). Available at: https://www.gov.uk/government/statistics/special-educational- needs-in-england-january-2015, p. 1.
7. Department for Education and Department of Health, *Special educational needs and disability code of practice: 0 to 25 years: Statutory guidance for organisations which work with and support children and young people who have special educational needs or disabilities* (2015). Available at: https://www.gov.uk/government/publications/ send-code-of-practice-0-to-25, p. 285.
8. Ministry of Justice and Youth Justice Board for England and Wales, *Youth custody report: March 2016*. Available at: https://www.gov.uk/government/statistics/ youth-custody-data.

Bibliography

Barrett, D. (2015). 'Disruptive pupils "hidden" by school during Ofsted visit'. *The Telegraph* (13 February). Available at: http://www.telegraph.co.uk/education/11411290/Disruptive-pupils-hidden-by-school-during-Ofsted-visit.html.

BBC News (2012). 'Michael Gove on vocational qualifications changes' (31 January). Available at: http://www.bbc.co.uk/news/education-16808902.

BBC News (2014). 'Disabled man "could have been saved"' (12 December). Available at: http://www.bbc.co.uk/news/uk-england-oxfordshire-30441266.

BBC News (2015a). 'Connor Sparrowhawk inquest: Care unit death "contributed to by neglect"' (16 October). Available at: http://www.bbc.co.uk/news/uk-england-oxfordshire-34548638.

BBC News (2015b). 'Nicky Morgan announces "war on illiteracy and innumeracy"' (1 February). Available at: http://www.bbc.co.uk/news/uk-31079515.

Beck, A.T. (1976). *Cognitive therapies and emotional disorders*. New York: New American Library.

Bindmans (2014). 'Death of 18-year-old Connor Sparrowhawk was preventable' (24 February). Available at: http://www.bindmans.com/news-and-events/news-article/death-of-18-year-old-connor-sparrowhawk-was-preventable.

Bower, J. (2010). 'Consequences for whom?' *for the love of learning* [blog] (20 October). Available at: http://www.joebower.org/2010/10/consequences-for-whom.html.

Brooks, G. (2010). 'Professor Greg Brooks critiques the government's proposed decoding test for 6 year olds'. Available at: https://ukla.org/news/story/professor_greg_brooks_critiques_the_governments_proposed_decoding_test_for.

Buchanan, M. (2015). 'NHS trust "failed to investigate hundreds of deaths"', *BBC News* (10 December). Available at: http://www.bbc.co.uk/news/health-35051845.

Busby, E. (2015). 'Exclusive: Brighter pupils make getting top ratings easier, Ofsted admits', *Times Educational Supplement* (21 November). Available at: https://www.tes.com/news/school-news/breaking-news/exclusive-brighter-pupils-make-getting-top-ratings-easier-ofsted.

Café, R. (2012). 'Winterbourne View: Abuse footage shocked nation', *BBC News* (26 October). Available at: http://www.bbc.co.uk/news/uk-england-bristol-20084254.

Care Quality Commission (2016a). *Ratings*. Available at: http://www.cqc.org.uk/content/ratings.

Care Quality Commission (2016b). *Southern Health NHS Foundation Trust Quality Report*. Available at: http://www.cqc.org.uk/sites/default/files/new_reports/AAAF4191.pdf.

Chatzitheochari, S., Parsons, S. and Platt, L. (2014). *Bullying experiences among disabled children and young people in England: Evidence from two longitudinal studies.* Department of Quantitative Social Science, Institute of Education, University of London. Available at: http://repec.ioe.ac.uk/REPEc/pdf/qsswp1411.pdf.

Cherrylkd (2015). 'Secure children's homes. A guest interview with @richardalbery84', *Cherrylkd –SEN Advocate* [blog]. Available at: https://cherrylkd.wordpress.com/2015/01/07/secure-childrens-homes-a-guest-interview-with-richardalbery84/.

Clark, A. (1993). *Alan Clark Diaries: In Power 1983–1992.* London: Weidenfeld & Nicolson.

Contact a Family (2013). *Falling through the net. Illegal exclusions, the experiences of families with disabled children in England and Wales (2013).* Available at: http://www.cafamily.org.uk/media/639982/falling_through_the_net_-_illegal_exclusions_report_2013_web.pdf.

Coughlan, S. (2015). 'Tory resit plan for pupils with poor SATs results', *BBC News* (8 April). Available at: http://www.bbc.co.uk/news/education-32204578.

Daulby, J. (2015). 'Mother Courage of the Reading Wars', *MainstreamSEND* [blog] (1 April). Available at: https://mainstreamsen.wordpress.com/2015/04/01/mother-courage-of-the-reading-wars/.

Department for Education (2011). *Teachers' Standards.* Available at: https://www.gov.uk/government/publications/teachers-standards.

Department for Education (2012). *Exclusion from maintained schools, Academies and pupil referral units in England: A guide for those with legal responsibilities in relation to exclusion.* Available at: https://www.gov.uk/government/uploads/system/uploads/attachment_data/file/269681/Exclusion_from_maintained_schools__academies_and_pupil_referral_units.pdf.

Department for Education (2015a). *Permanent and Fixed Period Exclusions in England: 2013 to 2014.* Available at: https://www.gov.uk/government/collections/statistics-exclusions.

Department for Education (2015b). *Special educational needs in England: January 2015.* Available at: https://www.gov.uk/government/statistics/special-educational-needs-in-england-january-2015.

Department for Education (2015c). 'Special needs expert to head new assessment review' [Press release]. Available at: https://www.gov.uk/government/news/special-needs-expert-to-head-new-assessment-review.

Department for Education (2015d). *Statistical First Release, Special educational needs in England: January 2015.* Available at: https://www.gov.uk/government/uploads/system/uploads/attachment_data/file/447917/SFR25-2015_Text.pdf.

Department for Education (2016a). *Educational Excellence Everywhere.* Available at: https://www.gov.uk/government/publications/educational-excellence-everywhere.

Department for Education (2016b). *Progress 8 measure in 2016, 2017, and 2018: Guide for maintained secondary schools, academies and free schools.* Available at: https://www.gov.uk/government/uploads/system/uploads/attachment_data/file/415486/Progress_8_school_performance_measure.pdf.

Department for Education and Department of Health (2015). *Special educational needs and disability code of practice: 0 to 25 years: Statutory guidance for organisations which work with and support children and young people who have special educational needs or disabilities.* Available at: https://www.gov.uk/government/publications/send-code-of-practice-0-to-25.

Department for Education and Nicky Morgan (2015). 'Nicky Morgan: one nation education' [speech]. Policy Exchange, London, 3 November. Available at: https://www.gov.uk/government/speeches/nicky-morgan-one-nation-education.

Department for Education and the Standards and Testing Agency (2015). *Statutory guidance: Phonics screening check.* Available at: https://www.gov.uk/government/publications/key-stage-1-assessment-and-reporting-arrangements-ara/phonics-screening-check#how-results-will-be-used-by-the-department-for-education-and-ofsted.

Dyson, A., Farrell, P., Polat, F., Hutcheson, G. and Gallannaugh, F. (2004). *Inclusion and Pupil Achievement.* London: Department for Education and Skills. Research Report RR578. Available at: http://webarchive.nationalarchives.gov.uk/20130401151715/http://www.education.gov.uk/publications/eOrderingDownload/RR578.pdf.

Emerson, E. and Hatton, C. (2007). *The Mental Health of Children and Adolescents with Learning Disabilities in Britain.* Lancaster University/Foundation for People with Learning Disabilities. Available at: http://www.lancaster.ac.uk/staff/emersone/FASSWeb/Emerson_07_FPLD_MentalHealth.pdf.

Flannagan, A. (2006). 'Tarred with the same brush', *The Guardian* (8 May). Available at: http://www.theguardian.com/uk/2006/may/08/ukcrime.immigrationpolicy.

Glover, G. and Ayub, M. (2010). *How People with Learning Disabilities Die.* Improving Health and Lives: Learning Difficulties Observatory. Available at: https://www.improvinghealthandlives.org.uk/uploads/doc/vid_9033_IHAL2010-06%20Mortality.pdf.

Henshaw, P. (2015). 'Schools willing to sacrifice outstanding grade over EBacc', *SecEd* (25 June). Available at: http://www.sec-ed.co.uk/news/schools-willing-to-sacrifice-outstanding-grade-over-ebacc.

Herrington, V. (2005). 'Meeting the healthcare needs of offenders with learning disabilities', *Learning Disability Practice*, 8(4): 28–32.

HMIC (2015). 'Peel assessments'. Available at: https://www.justiceinspectorates.gov.uk/hmic/peel-assessments/peel-2015/.

Hughes, A.G. and Hughes, E.H. (1947). *Learning and Teaching – an Introduction to Psychology and Education.* London: Longmans, Green & Co.

Human Rights Watch (2015). *'Complicit in Exclusion': South Africa's Failure to Guarantee an Inclusive Education for Children with Disabilities.* Available at: https://www.hrw.org/report/2015/08/18/complicit-exclusion/south-africas-failure-guarantee-inclusive-education-children.

Kohn, A. (1996). *Beyond Discipline: From compliance to community.* Alexandria, VA: Association for Supervision and Curriculum Development.

Lennox, C. and Khan, L. (2012). 'Youth justice'. In *Our Children Deserve Better: Prevention Pays*, the Annual Report of the Chief Medical Officer 2012. Available at: https://www.gov.uk/government/uploads/system/uploads/attachment_data/file/252662/33571_2901304_CMO_Chapter_12.pdf.

Lindsay, G. and Dockrell, J. (2010). *The relationship between speech, language and communication needs (SLCN) and behavioural, emotional and social difficulties (BESD)*. Department for Education Research Report DFE-RR247-BCRP6. Available at: https://www.gov.uk/government/uploads/system/uploads/attachment_data/file/219632/DFE-RR247-BCRP6.pdf.

Lortie, D. (1975). *Schoolteacher: A Sociological Study*. London: Chicago University Press.

Loucks, N. (2007). *No One Knows – offenders with learning difficulties and learning disabilities – review of prevalence and associated needs*. Prison Reform Trust. Available at: http://www.ohrn.nhs.uk/resource/policy/NoOneKnowPrevalence.pdf.

Mansell, J. (2010). *Raising Our Sights: services for adults with profound intellectual and multiple disabilities*. Mencap. Available at: https://www.mencap.org.uk/sites/default/files/documents/Raising_our_Sights_report.pdf.

Mazars (2015). *Independent review of deaths of people with a Learning Disability or Mental Health problem in contact with Southern Health NHS Foundation Trust April 2011 to March 2015*. Available at: https://www.england.nhs.uk/south/wp-content/uploads/sites/6/2015/12/mazars-rep.pdf.

McGauran, A. (2015). 'Parents question inspectors' special needs training', *Schools Week* (17 April). Available at: http://schoolsweek.co.uk/parents-question-inspectors-special-needs-training/.

McGaw, S. (2000). *What Works for Parents with Learning Disabilities?* Barnardo's. Available at: http://www.barnardos.org.uk/wwparwld.pdf.

McInerney, L. (2015). 'Top Ofsted rating for many SEN schools – so why aren't we trumpeting success?' *The Guardian* (20 January). Available at: http://www.theguardian.com/education/2015/jan/20/ofsted-sen-schools-outstanding.

Mencap (2015). 'Employment and training'. Available at: https://www.mencap.org.uk/get-involved/campaigns/what-we-campaign-about/employment-and-training.

Mental Disability Advocacy Centre (MDAC) and the United Nations Partnership on the Rights of Persons with Disabilities (2015). *The human rights of people with mental or intellectual impairments in the Republic of Moldova*. Available at: http://www.mdac.org/sites/mdac.info/files/moldova_report_2015_english.pdf.

Ministry of Justice and Youth Justice Board for England and Wales (2016), *Youth custody report: March 2016*. Available at: https://www.gov.uk/government/statistics/youth-custody-data.

Mottram, P. and Lancaster, R. (2006). *HMPs Liverpool, Styal and Hindley YOI: Preliminary Results*. Cumbria and Lancashire: NHS Specialised Services Commissioning Team.

Mottram, P.G. (2007). *HMP Liverpool, Styal and Hindley Study Report*. Liverpool: University of Liverpool. Available at: https://www.choiceforum.org/docs/hmpliverpool.pdf.

Nisbett, R. (2015). *Mindware: Tools for Smart Thinking*. London: Penguin.

O'Brien, J. (2014). 'Entitlement? Yes. Inclusion? No.' *Jarlath O'Brien* [blog] (30 December). Available at: https://jarlathobrien.wordpress.com/2014/12/30/entitlement-yes-inclusion-no/.

O'Brien, J. (2015). 'Five ways for heads to turn governors into a critical friend', *Times Educational Supplement* (8 October). Available at: https://www.tes.com/news/school-news/breaking-views/five-ways-heads-turn-governors-a-critical-friend.

O'Brien, J. (2016). 'White Paper: How SEND is the Achilles' heel of mass academisation', *TES* [blog] (27 March). Available at: https://www.tes.com/news/school-news/breaking-views/white-paper-how-send-achilles-heel-mass-academisation.

Office for National Statistics (2015). 'The latest on the UK labour market: March 2015 to May 2015'. Available at: http://www.ons.gov.uk/ons/rel/lms/labour-market-statistics/july-2015/sty-labour-market-statistics--july-2015.html.

Office of the Children's Commissioner (2013). *'Always Someone Else's Problem': Office of the Children's Commissioner's Report on illegal exclusions*. London: Office of the Children's Commissioner. Available at: http://www.childrenscommissioner.gov.uk/sites/default/files/publications/Always_Someone_Elses_Problem.pdf.

Office of the Children's Commissioner (2014). *'It might be best if you looked elsewhere': an investigation into the schools admission process*. Available at: https://www.childrenscommissioner.gov.uk/sites/default/files/publications/It_might_be_best_if_you_looked_elsewhere.pdf.

Ofsted (2009). *Twelve Outstanding Special Schools: Excelling through inclusion*. Available at: http://dera.ioe.ac.uk/11217/1/Twelve%20outstanding%20special%20schools%20-%20Excelling%20through%20inclusion.pdf.

Ofsted (2014). *The Annual Report of Her Majesty's Chief Inspector of Education, Children's Services and Skills 2013/14*. Available at: https://www.gov.uk/government/uploads/system/uploads/attachment_data/file/384699/Ofsted_Annual_Report_201314_HMCI_commentary.pdf.

Ofsted (2015a). *Monthly management information: Ofsted's school inspections outcomes*. Available at: https://www.gov.uk/government/statistics/monthly-management-information-ofsteds-school-inspections-outcomes.

Ofsted (2015b). *School inspection handbook: Handbook for inspecting schools in England under section 5 of the Education Act 2005* (August). Available at: https://www.gov.uk/government/publications/school-inspection-handbook-from-september-2015.

Ofsted (2015c). *The Annual Report of Her Majesty's Chief Inspector of Education, Children's Services and Skills 2014/15*. Available at: https://www.gov.uk/government/uploads/system/uploads/attachment_data/file/483347/Ofsted_annual_report_education_and_skills.pdf.

Ofsted (2015d). *Inspecting schools: handbook for inspectors*. Available at: https://www.gov.uk/government/publications/school-inspection-handbook.

Ravitch, D. (2014). 'Confessions of a teacher in a "no excuses" charter school'. *Diane Ravitch's Blog* [blog] (27 March). Available at: http://dianeravitch.net/2014/03/27/confessions-of-a-teacher-in-a-no-excuses-charter-school/.

Schools Week (2015). '*Schools Week* editor interviews Education Secretary, Nicky Morgan' [audio recording] (18 May). Available at: http://schoolsweek.co.uk/schools-week-editor-interviews-edcuation-secretary-audio-recording/.

Scott, S. (2015). 'The key points from the Department for Education's pupil projection figures', *Schools Week* (22 July). Available at: http://schoolsweek.co.uk/the-key-points-from-the-department-for-educations-pupil-projection-figures/.

Shaw, B., Bernardes, E., Trethewey, A. and Menzies, L. (2016). *Special educational needs and their links to poverty*. Joseph Rowntree Foundation. Available at: https://www.lkmco. org/wp-content/uploads/2016/02/Special-educational-needs-and-their-links-to-poverty.pdf.

Shipman, T. and Griffiths, S. (2015). 'All children must learn times tables', *The Sunday Times* (31 January). Available at: http://www.thesundaytimes.co.uk/sto/news/article1513958.ece?CMP=OTH-gnws-standard-2015_01_31.

Snowling, M., Nash, H. and Henderson, L. (2008). 'The development of literacy skills in children with Down syndrome: Implications for intervention'. Available at: https://www.down-syndrome.org/reviews/2066/.

Still, K. (2015). 'What % of outstanding schools have below average ability intake?' *KristianStill/Blog* [blog] (4 March). Available at: http://www.kristianstill.co.uk/wordpress/2015/03/04/what-of-outstanding-schools-have-below-average-ability-intake/.

TES (2015). 'Wilshaw and DfE on EBac collision course' (25 September). Available at: https://www.tes.com/news/school-news/breaking-news/wilshaw-and-dfe-ebac-collision-course.

Vanier, J. (2008). *Becoming Human*. Mahwah, NJ: Paulist Press.

Index